I'm *Only* Bleeding

Studies in the
Postmodern Theory of Education

Joe L. Kincheloe and Shirley R. Steinberg
General Editors

Vol. 10

PETER LANG
New York • Washington, D.C./Baltimore
Bern • Frankfurt am Main • Berlin • Vienna • Paris

Alan A. Block

I'm *Only* Bleeding

Education as the Practice of Social Violence Against Children

PETER LANG
New York • Washington, D.C./Baltimore
Bern • Frankfurt am Main • Berlin • Vienna • Paris

Library of Congress Cataloging-in-Publication Data

Block, Alan A.
I'm only bleeding: education as the practice of social violence against children/
Alan A. Block.
p. cm. —(Counterpoints: vol. 10)
Includes bibliographical references and index.
1. Education—Social aspects—United States. 2. Object relations
(Psychoanalysis)—United States. 3. Child development—United States.
4. Curriculum planning—United States. 5. Curriculum change—United States.
6. Postmodernism and education—United States. I Title. II. Series:
Counterpoints (New York, NY); vol. 10.
LC191.4.B56   370.19'24'0973—dc20   96-31810
ISBN 0-8204-2684-9
ISSN 1058-1634

Die Deutsche Bibliothek-CIP-Einheitsaufnahme

Block, Alan A.
I'm only bleeding: education as the practice of social violence against children/
Alan A. Block. –New York; Washington, D.C./Baltimore; Bern; Frankfurt am
Main; Berlin; Vienna; Paris: Lang.
(Counterpoints; Vol. 10)
ISBN 0-8204-2684-9
NE: GT

Excerpts from Robert Hunter's lyrics to the Garcia/Hunter composition
"Ripple" is reprinted by the kind permission of Ice Nine Publishing Company,
Inc. Excerpts from Bob Dylan's lyrics from "It's alright Ma (I'm Only
Bleeding)" reprinted by the kind permission of Special Rider Music, 1993.
Copyright Warner Bros. Publishing Company, 1965, Renewed Special Rider,
1993. Excerpts from Bob Dylan's lyrics from "When I Paint My Masterpiece"
is reprinted by the kind permission of Special Rider Music. Copyright Dwarf
Publishing Company, 1968. Excerpts from Bob Dylan's lyrics from "Like a
Rolling Stone" is reprinted by the kind permission of Special Rider Music.
Copyright Warner Bros. Publishing Company, 1965, Special Rider, 1993.

The paper in this book meets the guidelines for permanence and durability
of the Committee on Production Guidelines for Book Longevity
of the Council of Library Resources.

Printed in the United States of America.

Acknowledgments

I am hopelessly indebted to Joe Kincheloe and Shirley Steinberg (and Shirley Steinberg and Joe Kincheloe) whose confidence in me made the exploration which is this book possible. Their own work in education has been invaluable to the field and I have drawn heavily on·their scholarship and their friendship.

This project began with the financial backing of Dean Edwin Biggerstaff of the School of Education and Human Services at the University of Wisconsin-Stout. I am grateful for his support.

I thank my colleagues at the University of Wisconsin-Stout for putting up with my intrusion into their offices for the exploration of ideas or for the theft of chocolate candies. I have consumed incredible quantities of both sense and sweets in the writing of this book; my friends gave selflessly. I especially thank my dear confederate Amy Gillett who not only fed me candies but discussed them with me as well. Much tension was relieved and not a few ideas shared in these conversations. Of course, a great deal of chocolate was consumed in the process. My chair Dr. Don Stephenson supported the writing of this book with great humor and tremendous patience.

Portions of this book were read by others and I am grateful for their assistance. I thank especially Alflorence Cheatham and James Kiley who were kind enough to read the entire manuscript—sometimes several times—and whose input has proven invaluable. Barbara Standaert was kind enough to read and comment upon Chapter Six. I thank her as well. Jeanne Brady listened to me complain often about the writing; her friendship, patience and concern helped me through difficult times. Jeanne Kussrow-Larson proofread finished copies of the manuscript and is no longer concerned with the threat of senility.

This work in fact began in a chair in Barbara Kane's apartment office. There we talked a lot about children and about one child in particular.

Finally, my wife, Beth Peck, has lived with me through the wonder of this writing. I thank her.

Dedication

To my parents, Sidney David and Roberta Hirsh Block, who raised this child; to my wife, Beth Peck; and to Emma and Anna Rose, our children, whom we love.

Table of Contents

Violence is to be found in any action in which one acts as if one were alone to act: as if the rest of the universe were there only to receive the action . . .

Emmanuel Levinas

I shall not first give an historical survey and show the development of my ideas from the theories of others, because my mind does not work that way. What happens is that I gather this and that, here and there, settle down to clinical experience, form my own theories, and then, last of all, interest myself to see where I stole what. Perhaps this is as good a method as any.

D.W. Winnicott

Chapter I

It's Alright, Ma (I'm Only Bleeding)

The Bob Dylan song from which I have drawn the title of this chapter portrays a world in which human values are experienced as perverse, debased, and dangerous. When I ask who it is in the lyric who speaks of the phenomenal world in this manner it is the child-narrator to whom I must listen. It is he who speaks in this song. The world inscribed in the lyrics is one in which children are *self*-defined as at risk; this is a world in which hope is absent: the child cries that "There is no sense in trying" and then speaks comfortingly but ironically, "So don't fear, if you hear/A foreign sound to your ear/It's alright Ma, I'm only sighing." Now, I am not suggesting that we adults must accept this worldview simply because it is spoken, although admittedly across the political spectrum there is consensus concerning not only the child's risk but the world's endangered condition. However, I think it is necessary that we acknowledge the source of this dread in the child. For from the song's title and its anaphoric phrase, "It's alright, ma," I assume the speaker to be the child who, ironically, must tender solace to the caregiver for the child's experience of abuse: "It's alright, ma (I'm only bleeding)." In the song the child-narrator speaks of a world oppressed by a "darkness at the break of noon," of a world endangered by "disillusioned words [which] like bullets bark," of a world tyrannized by "money [which] doesn't talk, it swears obscenity," and of a world tenanted by those who "cultivate their flowers to be nothing more than something they invest in." It is a world in which the child ought to expect support, sustenance, even guidance, but in which the perceived hypocrisy and hate that organize his experience result in a reality that slips continually away, making ever more tenuous the nurturance, even the survival, of the child. What other interpretation would explain the graphic portrayal of a hostile world and the yet repeated reassurance from the child that "it's alright, ma"? For the narrator, survival in the face of this social violence is perceived as a perilous condition that leads, at best, to a wounded existence: it's alright, ma, I'm only bleeding.

And the world portrayed here is a world in which reality is framed and supported by a complicitous educational system where, in the words of the child, "Teachers teach that knowledge waits/Can lead to hundred dollar plates." The menacing values of the daily world are understood as the substantive materials of the school; the very essence of school seems to have no relationship to the child's immediate life nor, indeed, much connection to anything but a corrupt and limiting world outside the school. In this portrayal the very identity of the child—the production, presence, and awareness of knowledge—rests, says the educational system, not in the child's own activities, but in that which exists outside the child and which must be embedded within often, as we will argue, by abusive force. Yet the child-narrator of the song knows that beyond him is a world, ma, whose social systems offer not only little support for growth but which even imperil the child's survival. The world Dylan portrays in the song is characterized by systems in which social violence against the child are strikingly depicted as deriving from the very systems into which the child is educated to contribute. It is a world in which the child's growth becomes a function of the violence that the world, in the form of its systems, exercises upon the child and in which the practice of education is centrally and actively complicitous.

Dylan's song "It's Alright, Ma (I'm Only Bleeding)" is a song that speaks of the child's experience of pain in a world depicted as physically and morally ignoble. It is a world in which the child is assailed by forces over which s/he has little control and which in its moral stance sets itself off as the child's adversary; in this world the child is conceptualized as the stranger whose dubious social stature requires vigilant action by the adults. The world represented in the song is a world in which moral values exercise a form of social violence resulting in the tenuousness of not only the child's physical survival but his/her psychological existence as well. Indeed, in the words of the song, the continued survival of the child is endangered even by the child's own self-generated thoughts and visions, the very origin of his creativity and identity: "If my thought dreams could be seen, they'd probably put my head in a guillotine," the narrator cries as he resignedly notes, "But it's alright, ma, it's life and life only." Bob Dylan portrays an existential world in which the child might have hoped for the possibility of creating him/herself but for society's order to wait for Godot at some nondescript barren location–the school– and for no apparent reason except that Godot has given the child the order to do so. It is that order and that place with which this book deals, for that order and that place seem to me to deny our children the promise of education and the growth that it should hearten, denies the child the possibility of growth and the education that should accompany and promote it. This book discusses the violence committed against the child in the name of education and suggests that the title of Dylan's song is the yet relevant and plaintive cry of the wounded child.

I do not mean to discuss the evident violence that surrounds children in their physical environments shaped by poverty and its product, the violence that is described so painfully in the works of Jonathan Kozol, first in *Death at an Early Age* (1967) and more recently in *Savage Inequalities* (1991) or *Amazing Grace* (1995). Nor will I speak specifically of the violence of the streets that denies the very identity of what we have come to know as children. Psychologists such as James Garbarino (1991) speak eloquently on this topic. These would be obviously painful accounts but ones from which we might disingenuously and self-righteously distance ourselves. We could say, that is not our home: I am not part of that crime. Rather, I would like to discuss the violence that is practiced upon the child psychologically by the educational system that presently functions in the United States and that consequently denies the development of self and world which is the birthright of every individual in our society and which ought to be the primary activity of every person. It is a system of which we are all a product, a system whose violence has left us all, perhaps, bleeding even as it has taught us how to wound. But it is a system that has inured us to our roles, made bleeding so common that it is not seen as irregular, but rather, as evidence of the real.

I live with two young children, and I have taught thousands
more; I have even once been a child myself, probably in many
ways I still am so. I am surrounded, in fact, by children.[1] I
mean, these children confront me daily—I live with them; they
sit before and beside me. They demand of me, demand that I
listen and demand that I speak. I am supposed to teach them;
I know they want very much to learn, "Daddy, what is that
name?" my twenty-two-month-old daughter asks. I answer her
with gentleness, with immediacy, and with seriousness. I am
prepared for her next question. Or for that of her six-year-old
sister. I am prepared for *her*. But in the schools, our children
and their teachers are constrained by structures and methods
and bodies of knowledge that have been previously devised
and approved by someone whom the children (and often the
teachers) do not know and who has never bothered to make
their acquaintance. I do not think our children may count on
the kindness of these strangers who are not, indeed, strangers
for the children but are, rather, estranged from them. These
(e)strangers will never know "what is that name" because they
are not present—for lack of time or space or vision—to see the
pointing finger or the inquiring visage. Rather, as educators
we are told that there is knowledge that these children need
and that must be communicated; we are supposed to assume
that this must be true for we have been told by *them* that it is
true! We are counseled that the country's future rests on the
success of the children's learning and of my teaching. There is
a hierarchy in which we exist and to which we owe allegiance;
this hierarchy must be followed if the order is to be maintained.
The children, too, are obliged to these hierarchies. Indeed, as
I will suggest, they are defined by these very hierarchies. There
are techniques to deal with and classifications to assign to students with whom I have trouble and who have trouble learning
what I have to teach using the methods I was taught. I am not
comforted. It's alright, ma, I'm only bleeding.

But I cannot keep from wondering: For whom were these
hierarchies and methods devised? How have these children

---

[1] I am grateful to David Jardine (1988a) who reminds me that Piaget
found studying children so easy because "there are children all around us."
I mean to problematize the distinction between children and us even as
Jardine called into question Piaget's use of the generic child.

before us been conceptualized that this is the education they receive? Who are these children, I ask, who sit before us? What are they meant to learn? "They" may be all around us, but who exactly are "they"? And how do we know who "they" are? How did "they" get this definition? And if we do not know *for sure* what it is we do and to whom we do it, isn't it possible—even probable—that what we do in the exercise of education may be a form of violence? I cannot keep from reflecting upon the emergence of the identity of the child upon whom these methods are practiced and the identity of that child after these educational experiences. I cannot keep from considering how these children have been conceptualized that they are expected to elide through the educational system acquiring . . . well acquiring what, I wonder? And becoming what, I wonder? And prepared to enter what world, I ask? I wonder because I would let no one ignore my children's individualities for that of the generic child; I would not permit their classification by an educational system. I cannot classify them myself for risk of denying them and subsequently denying me as well.

It is clear that children are, as are we all, products of the historical moment; as Marx said in *The Eighteenth Brumaire of Louis Bonaparte* (1984, 15), "Men make their own history, but they do not make it just as they please; they do not make it under circumstances chosen by themselves, but under circumstances directly encountered, given and transmitted from the past." What a child is results from the historical circumstances from which the child's definition derives. I do not choose these times, but like Estragon in Beckett's *Waiting for Godot* "I know where I am." Although we may live in postmodern times,[2] I believe the schools define my children by the spirit of modernity—a period when order and classification were values prioritized by and in the social world. Indeed, not only were these values given priority, they defined that world as well. Outside of order the world ceased to exist. The ordering and bureaucratizing of the American public schools is a well-documented narrative (Nasaw 1979; Katz 1987; Reimer 1971; Kliebard 1987) and may be attributed to the moments of modernity.

---

[2] I am aware that postmodernism is both a description and a critique. I mean it here as a description.

The exact dating of modernity is unclear, but Zygmunt Bauman (1991, 4) suggests that it might be described as (a) a cultural project deriving from at least the Enlightenment but perhaps from as early as the fourteenth century and; (b) a "socially conscious way of life." The modernity that defines our children, and the education that stems from that modernity and that will condition our children, organizes the society into which they are meant to enter even as that modernity organizes the consciousness by which society is organized. In his study *Ambivalence and Modernity*, Bauman (1991, 7) argues that modernity arose as a product of the human quest for certainty and as methods and technologies of measurement and categorization made the possibility of the achievement of certainty seem attainable. This vision of the Enlightenment was a vision of the ideal, and the daily world was subsequently designed to accomplish that ideal. Bauman (1991, 37) writes:

> One could almost say with the vision of hindsight that the vision of the Enlightenment was made to respond to dreams and cravings of East-European political visionaries—intellectuals and, more generally, 'educated classes'. No other social location was more perfectly reflected in the imagery of the social ideal standing ahead of social reality and pulling it forward; in the vision of society as pliable raw material to be moulded and brought into proper shape by architects armed with a proper design; in the image of society incapable, if left to its own course, of either improving itself or even comprehending what the improvement would look like; in the concept of knowledge as power, reason as the judge of reality and an authority entitled to dictate and enforce the *ought* over the *is*.

The *modern* is a world organized by the creation of order by the rational sciences and the positivistic science of philosophy (see Dewey, *The Quest of Certainty*). Its ideal is self-derived and its practices—including that of education–are based on that exemplary but impossible image.

Order is the quintessential governing principle of the modern. Indeed, the modern creates the very idea of order; Bauman argues that the modern creates itself out of nothing but its own designing impulse. That is, modernity does not create a world out of something, but rather produces it out of nothing; without the designing impulse of modernity, nothing would be there. The Other of modernity is chaos. The development of the modern takes place amidst the growing advances of the classifying sciences; and since classification attempts to deny ambivalence, then it is only with more classification that ambivalence can be resisted. The hierarchy continues to expand. Modernity may be defined by the actions of agencies that make out of chaos order.

> We can say that existence is modern in as far as it is effected and sustained by *design, manipulation, management, engineering*. The existence is modern in as far as it is administered by resourceful (that is, possessing knowledge, skill and technology), sovereign agencies. Agencies are sovereign in as far as they claim and successfully defend the right to manage and administer existence: the right to define order and, by implication, lay aside chaos, as that left-over that escapes definition (Bauman, 1991, 7, emphasis in original).

Ambivalence is the by-product of chaos. Ambivalence confuses certainty and renders it unattainable. And modernity is organized to deny ambivalence and avoid doubt. Children, however, enact the embodiment of ambivalence. They will not be contained in our definitions. They must be categorized. David Smith (1988, 175) writes that "The most remarkable thing about contemporary North American teacher education may be that, in the name of concern for children, we have banished children, themselves rightful persons in the total human drama, under a dense cover of rationalistic, abstract discourse about 'cognition,' 'development,' 'achievement,' etc." As Dylan says in another context, "Lord, protect my child."

It is as a product of this rage for order that the social world comes to be organized into the clear binary categories of friend and enemy. "Friends and enemies stand in opposition to each other. The first are what the second are not, and vice versa," writes Bauman (1991, 53). "The enemies are the negativity to the friends' positivity. The enemies are what the friends are not. The enemies are flawed friends; they are the *wilderness* that violates friends' *homeliness*, the *absence* which is a denial of friends' *presence*." But children cannot be so summarily categorized as either friend or enemy: they live amongst us but not among us; they are of us but not like us, Piaget tells us (see Jardine 1988a). In modernity, however, what escapes classification threatens the general order and must be dealt with. Neither friend nor enemy, the stranger as category enacts the unclassifiable and must therefore be administered and managed for the good of the order. The movement of modernity may be understood in part as the attempt to handle strangers and strangerhood. "Since the sovereignty of the modern intellect is the power to define and to make the definitions stick—everything that eludes unequivocal allocation is an anomaly and a challenge" (Bauman 1991, 9). Children in their unwillingness to be contained by definition threaten the order and must be dealt with as strangers to that order.

It has been the practice of the modern world to offer to the stranger assimilation as a means of social entry. Assimilation, however—the theoretical, educationally based activity by which the outsider becomes the insider, the invitation by which the stranger becomes either a friend or an enemy—is, interestingly, an impossibility in the modern. First, the stranger is not self-defined but is constructed by the "natural order" of the defining mechanisms. What characterizes the "stranger" are the characteristics that are ascribed to it. It knows itself only by the definitions of others. Assimilation would hardly eliminate those intrinsic characteristics; rather, it would offer a set of manners and behavioral norms that would always be recognized as disguise. Furthermore, that which escapes the definitions would always identify the stranger as stranger; one cannot eliminate what is not seen. Second, the stranger is someone who forces his way "into [my] life-world *uninvited*, thereby casting me on the receiving side of his initiative, making me into the object of action of which he is the subject: all this . . . is the notorious mark of the enemy" (Bauman 1991, 59). However, this stranger, as Bauman notes, claims to be my friend; he will not be kept at a secure distance and threatens the binarism by which society is ordered into friends and enemies. The stranger, Bauman (1991, 59) asserts, "would expose the failing of the opposition itself. He is a constant threat to the world's order." The stranger who desires entry as a friend calls into question the very notion of the social structure and thus must be denied entrance. Assimilation is a blind alley. The child as stranger must be contained.

Bauman looks to the Jewish experience in Germany as the quintessential experience of the impossibility of assimilation. On the one hand, the Jew was indeed, defined by the non-Jew, who in the social world were the respectable persons and who had, therefore, the sole authority to define who or what was a Jew. "It was they and they alone who decided on the principle which enabled the Jew to set the bits and pieces of this 'Jewish material' into a meaningful pattern" (Bauman 1991, 89). On the other hand, the "assimilating Jews acted under the pressure to prove their Germanhood, yet the very attempt to prove it was held against them as the evidence of their duplicity, and in all probability, also of subversive intentions." That is, assimilation was not only defined by the German but denied by it as well. The Jew as stranger threatened the order and had to be eliminated. The Nazi holocaust, Bauman has written, is simply a product of modernity's logic.

We might understand the child as existing in a similar situation. It is adults who give the child form by the manner in which the child is defined: when I was a child I behaved like a child, but when I became an adult I threw off childish ways—as soon as someone told me what they were.[3] Given the developing structures of the school over the past several centuries as well as my experience in and with them over two and a half decades, I must acknowledge that my child—all children—seems to have been conceptualized as such a stranger, one who must be dealt with for the security of the order and of social stability. To the horror of the social order, our children will not be contained by its social practices; the child is understood as an anomaly. Thomas Kuhn (1970) has explored how anomalies are treated in science—discounted and ignored—until they become so overwhelming that they require a redefinition of the object, which is a reclassification of the very principles by which a thing is defined. Kuhn has referred to this process as a paradigm shift. It is a willed blindness that prevents such a revolution now regarding children. Jonathan Silin (1995) argues eloquently for the necessity of a paradigm shift regarding our understanding of the child; I do not believe we have yet begun that process.

I will suggest throughout this book, rather, that our educational system is organized by modernity and by modernity's quest to *deny* the ambivalence that the child presents to the

---

[3] Kurt Vonnegut (1969) writes that "Maturity is a disease for which laughter is the only cure, if laughter can be said to cure anything."

modern world—the Otherness of order that it epitomizes. In its desire to deny ambivalence, modernity must handle these anomalies or risk the chaos that would end the world as known. The modern child—like the educational system to which s/he is condemned—is a product of the ordering of the world in modernity. The crisis of the schools spoken of so glibly of late is a product not of the failure of schools but of the threat that the child poses to the project of modernity. The individual children in our classroom bespeak the centrality of ambivalence in our world and deny the very project of modernity: the permanent establishment of order. The schools themselves represent the social power to contain the stranger and avoid the uncertainty the child epitomizes. The child reminds us of the postmodern condition of ambivalence that so terrifies the ideologues of modernity and that they would prefer to scorn. As a result of his/her presence and the ambiguity to which s/he attests and for the good of the social order, the child must be set away both physically and psychologically. As the object of adult analysis, the child of modernity is rendered invisible by the drive to effect his/her regularity.

These are issues raised eloquently by David Jardine (1988a, 185) who writes: "The obviousness of the commonplace [that there are children all around us] poses the question of what it means to live in a world in which children are a potent presence in our lives. And in the sphere of education, we find that we must live with the question of what it is we wish to bring forth in children, and how we should proceed in doing this." This sense of wonderment that children inspire is the very substance of ambivalence that modernity desires desperately to deny. Jardine is himself troubled by the generic definitions that derive from Piaget's work and that order the child and his/her development. Modernity's response to the phenomenon of the child is to further classify it in an attempt to control the child, to make ever more careful delineations of the it and of the knowledge that s/he must learn and the mechanisms by which that knowledge may be acquired. For example, today we have not only adolescence—a category itself invented by G. Stanley Hall at the beginning of the present century—but early and late adolescence as well, each with its particular set of traits and each with its necessary pedagogy. The invention of the junior high school derives from the belief that different stages of human development require different types of education. Middle schools are a further extension of the classifying practices of modernity. The child is first defined into existence and then controlled by the very definitions that gave him/her existence. I would not treat my child in this fashion; neither, I hope, would I do so to other people's children.

What I would like to suggest is that the postmodern child represents the Other of order, the stranger to modernity, the ambivalence that modernity wishes to eliminate. The educational apparatus has been constructed to control the ambivalence that the child inspires. Ambivalence threatens the definite. Modernity is, argues Bauman (1991, 5), the time when the order "of the world, of the human habitat, of the human self, and of the connection between all three—is *reflected upon*; a matter of thought, of concern, of a practice that is aware of itself, conscious of being a conscious practice and wary of the void it would leave were it to halt or merely relent." The modern understands that order designed holds back chaos; order is socially contrived and is a matter of will. The child potentially threatens the order for, by definition, the child's desire is beyond the control of the adult, indeed, may not even be comprehended by the adult. In modernity, the individual and singular child not only comes into being as a product of that ordering, but the child's potential for chaos—its unintegration, to use Winnicott's description (1965, 1971, 1984, 1986)— endangers that order. That is, although our science has categorized the child into existence so does the individual child— my child and your child—threaten the order of the adult world, itself a product of adult categorization. Miss Watson may prohibit Huck his pipe but because she "done it herself" snuff is acceptable. The warnings of modernity are that the uncontrolled and ill-defined child left free would endanger the order of society. It is partly for this reason, as I will suggest later, that schools have been designed.

In modernity's project the definition of the child is made so precise that the imaginative freedom of the individual child is denied. The child's freedom to play and explore is severely curtailed for the good of the greater order. But to control play is to deny it and to therefore deny the child's discovery of meaning in the world. Jardine (1988b, 34) says that "Play is the exploration of possible worlds of meaning, an exploration of embeddedness in meaning and the creation and sustaining of such embeddedness. It is a free exploration . . . of possibilities of mutual understanding." There must be place and time provided for children's play. Play facilitates development. Development is the creation of self and subjectivity.

Marian Milner argues ([1950], 1990, 133) that the transition from childhood to adulthood requires the discovery of some place in the social world to which one might dedicate one's energies. One must discover what Milner refers to as "the gap in the world" into which one can pour one's imagination. Play takes place in that gap and might be considered the creation of the frame—that which separates the outside world from the world of the imagination. That frame marks off the personal world from the public one. It distinguishes between the world outside the frame, which may not be adjusted, and that within, which is a product of the imagination working on the world outside. Indeed, the frame permits perception of the canvas so that a painting might be produced, but the frame itself is a creative act that depends for its existence on the materials from the external world. That is, the frame makes possible empty space in which play might occur. But play requires objects and these must derive from the material world. And in play the frame acknowledges the outside world but makes imaginative creation possible by creating that gap into which the energies might be inscribed. Play creates a world out of materials of this world that are available for such use. Play is creativity. Vygotsky (1978, 102) says that "Action in the imaginative sphere, in an imaginary situation, the creation of voluntary intentions, and the formation of real-life plans and volitional motives—all appear in play and make it the highest level of preschool development." In play the stick becomes a horse, but the child never denies that the horse is actually a stick. One must be permitted to create the frame that subsequently establishes the canvas. Without the frame there is no canvas on which to work; but without an external world there is no need of a canvas. To be enabled to create the frame—to invent the gap—requires first that one feel that the world wants what we have to give, that we might pour our creativity onto the canvas framed. My daughter talks of her dolls as if they were alive; I know they are for her and I respond accordingly. She knows that they are only dolls. My daughter has no desire to treat me as a doll.

But in its quest for order, modernity denies the possibility of creating the frame for the ready accessibility and the truth of prefabricated mass-produced ones. The canvases come already framed. Our children have only to paint by numbers. In the ordered society of modernity there are slots into which the individual might fit and definitions that organize both the child's experience and the child him/herself. The opposite is also true: definitions of the child organize the available experiences available to that child. Outside those definitions the child threatens the order and inspires further classification. See the burgeoning field of attention deficit disorder (ADD) and attention deficit hyperactivity disorder (ADHD) to discover the yet potent power of modernity. But Milner (1950/1990, 110) says, "trying to make a picture deliberately rather than by the free drawing method" was so difficult because it was so hard to keep the frame in mind. Huge gaps would appear on the canvas. That is, overdefinition—trying to get it right—denied creative freedom and artistic production.

I will explore the notion that the modern child comes into existence coincident with the invention of the modern school— that is, a school bent on order and ordering. If the principle of order (and ordering) is the principle of modernity, then the child threatens that order for the child is, finally, indefinable except from the perspectives of the adults for whom ordering establishes the world. And the order of adult society, Bauman argues, is established by the dichotomy of friend and enemy: "The friends/enemies opposition sets apart truth from falsity, good from evil, beauty from ugliness. It also differentiates between proper and improper, right and wrong, tasteful and unbecoming. It makes the world readable and thereby instructive. It dispels doubt"(Bauman 1991, 54). In this sense the child comes to be known as a stranger. The stranger disrupts the binarism that defines the modern: the stranger is neither a friend nor a foe—it is undecidable and makes action difficult. "Oppositions enable knowledge and action; undecidables paralyze them. Undecidables brutally expose the artifice, the fragility, the sham of the most vital of separations. They bring the outside into the inside, and poison the comfort of order with suspicion of chaos" (Bauman 1991, 56). The child is a stranger in the world of modernity: its undecidability threatens the oppositions that deny the ambivalence modernity wishes to eliminate. Joe Kincheloe (forthcoming) has written eloquently of the barely concealed hatred of the child evident in the popular media, such as the movie *Home Alone* and the smart-alecky children so evident on TV screens in the United States. The child may be invited into the world—but it is so, as I will later suggest, already called into being, already hailed an object in order to deny its position as stranger and to prevent it from disrupting the social order. Education has been structured by modernity to avoid the ambivalence that the child inevitably epitomizes. The unintegrated child threatens order and must be controlled. So, for example, the child's arrival becomes an historical event. The exact date of its arrival is gloriously preserved and each moment recorded for historical inscription. The ubiquitous camcorders are evidence of the documentation of the child's life—the child is an event in history rather than a natural event.[4] This book will explore the modern social order's response to the ambivalence that the child presents to the world.

There is another sense in which this book is concerned with the violence that the educational system commits on our children. And I do not mean to accuse our school workers as child-abusers, as demons or sadists. Rather, I suggest that the social structures outside the schools have grave consequences for the activity that takes place within them, for they promote a form of violence that might produce hopelessless and despair. This form of violence is a product of the prevailing American ideology upon which the school purports to be based and the reality of the world that actually exists. We are a society whose completion is always in the future; we are not as much con-

---

[4] I am struck of late by the centrality of the weather as a news item. Rather than accept the exigencies of climate, we have moved the weather to a primary news story as if the recent snowstorm were equivalent to the budget standoff or to the war in Bosnia. I am reminded of what William James said about climate: "Climate is really only the name for a certain group of days, but it is treated as if it lay *behind* the day, and in general, we place the name, as if it were a being, behind the facts it is the name of." The same is true for children: childhood becomes defined by our recording of it rather than its simply being itself.

cerned with the past as we are with the future. This is both our failure and our hope. I have argued elsewhere (Block 1995) that it is for this reason that behaviorism has rooted so firmly here; we deny the power of history in our present so that we may constantly remake ourselves anew. Our educational systems are organized to prepare our children for the ever-available future. But if the promise of the school lies in jobs and financial success, then what is the effect on our children when the future offers such limited possibilities for so many of them. What violence do we practice when we prepare them for the future that will never exist? "I hope we can begin to see what happens in our moment," Cornel West (1993, 42) states, "when a distinctive philosophical tradition of this country that puts such a premium on the future clashes with the breakdown in social systems of nurturing children in which their conception of the future narrows, hollows, and hence a moment in a very unique civilization and culture, in which the possibility, the sense of possibility, is more and more called into question." On the one hand, our society holds a narrower future than that for which we expect our school system to prepare our children. By the same token, in their practices our schools offer our children a limited future. The violence we practice on our children in the name of education creates a society of despair.

This book represents a promise made to my children and to the children who are my children's contemporaries. This book represents a promise to the children who never were children. This book represents a promise to the adults who were once children. David Purpel (1989, 93) writes that "Our culture's insistence on competition, individual success, and privatism is reflected in a school program which puts cultural considerations of achievement, order, control and hierarchy over educational values of free inquiry, the development of a critical and creative consciousness, and the struggle for meaning." This book promises that bleeding will no longer be accepted as a sign of the natural; that indeed, it is not alright, ma, that they are bleeding. It is not alright that we are bleeding. Rabbi Nachman of Bratslav said, "If you believe that you can damage, then believe that you can fix." This book is part of that belief. This book represents a part of that promise.

Chapter II

Object Relations:
Being, the Self, and the School

My daughter begins the first grade this year. She will, I hope, have wonderful teachers; I am not overly optimistic, though perhaps I yet have faith. She speaks of a persisting rumor that first grade is the end of school pleasure and the beginnings of school pain. From here on, my child claims, learning is serious and life is hard. There is homework. Snack time and nap time cease, to be replaced with seat time and worksheets. Reading becomes no longer a wonderful exploration but turns into a chore. Basal readers replace literature; learning to read replaces reading. Channel One is the news of the week in review; there will be no newspaper or magazine subscriptions in her classroom. School becomes business: in Beverly Cleary's novel, *Ramona, The Brave* (1975, 158), Beezus, Ramona's sister says of the teacher, "There wasn't anything really wrong with [Mrs. Griggs], I guess . . . she just wasn't very exciting is all. She wasn't mean or anything like that. We just seemed to go along doing our work, and that was it." But, yes, I believe that there is, indeed, something wrong with Mrs. Griggs, something very wrong with the system in which she worked. Education ought not to be just "going along doing our work, and that was it." Education should not, in fact, be so . . . well, so mundane.

Henry David Thoreau (1961, 60) tells us that as he traveled about he would regard the town where the "inhabitants were plainly cultivators of the earth, and lived under an organized political government. The schoolhouse stood with a meek aspect, entreating a long truce to war and savage life." Thoreau recognized that the schoolhouse was part of the culture of the town and it bespoke domesticity, husbandry, and mannered cultivation. Here was no place for exploration or wildness, a phrase by which Thoreau might mean our original passion. "Gardening is civil and social, but it wants the vigor and freedom of the forest and the outlaw" (1961, 61).[1] No, for Thoreau the timidity promulgated by the school was anathema to discovery and akin to the domestication that decried adventure and risk. Formal schooling was not agreeable to Henry David; its ties to organized cultivation and civilization led him to shun it: "I would at least strike my spade into the earth with such careless freedom but accuracy as the woodpecker his bill into a tree . . . What have I do to with plows? I cut another furrow than you see" (Thoreau 1961, 61). But schools, as Thoreau knew well and as Ramona Quimby soon learns, are replete with plows for cutting furrows. "What does education do," he asks, "but turn a meandering brook into a well cut ditch?" School culture does not bode well for that wildness that portends exploration and discovery. "A highly cultivated man," Thoreau (1961, 62) says contemptuously, is one "whose bones can be bent! whose heaven-born virtues are but good manners." For this cultivation schools provide the quintessential plow. I would not have this for my daughters. I am concerned with the availability and use of objects in the classrooms of formal education. I am concerned with the use of my daughter as an object and the availabilities of her own uses of objects—including herself—in the classrooms of her school. That potential for use and the actual uses of objects play an enormous role in the development of her selfhood and subjectivity.

This fall in my classroom at the university, I will meet my daughters and your sons in my classes in the teacher education program. They will be good students; they will be, as it were, cultivated. That is, they will be well-mannered; they will wait to find what it is I want and then give it to me. They will volunteer little, claiming shyness as their modus operandi; they will ask no difficult questions. They will accomplish only what is assigned and that most perfunctorily: they have already learned how not to read the texts and how to take tests. They will risk nothing. These future teachers will say: "Just tell me what to

---

[1] I am reminded of Bob Dylan's thought that "To live outside the law you must be honest."

do and I will do it. I will even do it well. Just please, don't give me any theory, don't ask me to think or ask me to reconsider the courses of my life. I just want to graduate and be a teacher."[2] At educational conferences frequented by classroom teachers, sessions that offer ready-made handouts are always well attended. How-to books are de rigueur in education classrooms. There are even whole language workbooks!! I tell my students, "A dear friend of mine once offered me a book titled *If You Meet the Buddha on the Side of the Road, Kill Him!!* As your friend I say to you: If you come across a whole language workbook, burn it!!" I despair. I am frightened for my daughter. And for all the other children in her class. I would not have them be so . . . well . . . cultivated.

You see, I know that school is important. No, school and the process of education are profound. But they are so for reasons apart from though yet connected to the agenda of the conservatives or the fundamentalist right. You see, it is not only what we teach there—though indeed that is crucial to the argument of the conservative agenda and therefore to mine as well (hence the often vicious argument over multicultural education); it is with schooling as a way of being and of coming to being, of relating to others and to the self and to knowledge with which I am concerned. I am concerned with objects and their uses (for an extended conversation regarding object use and curriculum see Grumet, 1988). Selfhood begins long before schooling, though perhaps schooling functions to repress this knowledge. Schooling, of which school is only part, is ultimately a process that is built upon, develops from, and involves relations with myriad objects. Finally, those objects require use. The use of objects makes possible the evocation of selfhood. Minimally, the school is a space—an object—that can be used for play and creativity. It is an environment that can be used to facilitate the development of the self. For the most part, and as the twentieth century labors for breath, school has become a training ground for business. Schooled to work is the achievement of the educated. This does not bode well for education.

---

[2] Here I am again called to popular culture and to Liza Doolittle's reproach to Freddy Eynsford-Hill's expressions of affection: "Don't talk of love, show me." In my classroom—and in those of many of my colleagues—it is talk of theory that is to be avoided: just show me.

It does not bode well for the development of self. "But unless we do more," Thoreau (1961, 150) says, "than simply learn the trade of our time, we are but apprentices, and not yet masters of the art of life." Many of my students—and so many of our children—will be always apprentices: apprentices in teaching and apprentices in life. As an environment, to use Winnicott's phrases, school is not so much facilitating as discouraging, not so much holding as confining. It does not provide space for the teachers to be good enough so that they might provide space for the education that is good enough for our children. The school's structures do not enable the good enough teacher to permit, much less facilitate, that development; rather, the school's structures choke off the ability to play and replace it with work. Education causes serious damage.

Martin Dysart, the psychiatrist in Peter Shaffer's play *Equus* (1973), sits at his desk despairing over his purpose. He is supposed to treat Alan Strang whose passion Dysart admires, though that passion under the pressure of social strictures and taboos has turned destructive. Dysart understands his social function, but he doubts his knowledge. He questions his purpose based on his inevitable ignorance.

> A child is born into a world of phenomena all equal in their power to enslave. It sniffs, it sucks—it strokes its eyes over the whole uncomfortable range. Suddenly one strikes. Why? Moments snap together like magnets forging a chain of shackles. Why? I can trace them. I can even, with time, pull them apart again. But why at the start they were ever magnetized at all—just those particular moments of experience and no others—I don't know. *And nor does anyone else.* Yet *if* I don't know—if I can never know that—then what am I doing here? I don't mean clinically doing or socially doing—I mean fundamentally! These Whys, are fundamental—yet they have no place in a consulting room. So then, do I? (p. 76)

Dysart's anguish stems from his knowledge that his purpose is to normalize Alan Strang, to take away his particular passion and make him like everyone else. "I'll set him on a nice mini-scooter and send it puttering off into the Normal world where animals are treated *properly*: made extinct, or put into servitude, or tethered all their lives in dim light, just to feed it! I'll give him the good Normal world where we're tethered beside them—blinking our nights away in a non-stop drench of cathode-ray over our shrivelling heads" (Shaffer 1973, 108). He will, Dysart acknowledges, cultivate Alan to be a cultivator of domesticated gardens. It is, after all, what Dysart is paid to do by a society which demands this socialization.

And yet serious doubts persist; Dysart confesses that despite his expertise and despite his knowledge he cannot in fact know what he actually does in that office. "In an ultimate sense I cannot know what I do in this place—yet I do ultimate things. Essentially I cannot know what I do—yet I do essential things. Irreversible, terminal things" (108). I hear in Dysart's anguished cries my fears concerning education in the United States. I think that what occur in schools are ultimate and essential things; irreversible and terminal things. I know. I have spent my entire life in schools. And like Dysart in his psychiatric office, I despair over the condition in the schools. I despair for our children. I despair for ourselves who must deny our children *as we ourselves have been and are denied now* the opportunity to gallop. We may explore no wildness. We spend too much time normalizing and too little time understanding. Dewey ([1902]/1956) had earlier suggested we return the curriculum to the child, but I think we have now lost sight of that child to whom we must bring the curriculum.

I will not—indeed, cannot—offer a panacea for the school tragedy presently acting out in our society. But I would like to explore for a time the occupants of that institution: those who enter these institutions. Perhaps if we better understood the lives of our children[3] we could for the next century invent a place where their education might be facilitated by good enough teachers. If we cannot know ultimately what we do in our classrooms, perhaps we can ultimately know what those classrooms might be about so that we can provide for the selves that occupy our classrooms an environment in which they might flourish. Indeed, it is time even to reconsider the meaning of "flourish." If we cannot know essentially what we do, perhaps we might understand what essential things we do. In civilization, Thoreau suggests, "man degenerates at length . . ." It ought not to be our purpose to be accomplices to that degeneracy.

---

[3] I borrow this wonderful phrase from George Dennison (1969) to whose work I owe a great deal.

Knowledge, it must be stated at the start, is not what we are about: knowledge does not exist without a knower. Education, rather, is the establishment of a relation between the knower and the known. In that relationship both are created. We must first understand, I think, the origin of self as the relationship between knower and known so that we might facilitate this growth in these relations. We come into being as a result of object relations; self is a product of object relations; subjectivity derives from conscious uses of objects. Being a character, a personality, is releasing our selves into available objects. Schools severely control the availability and use of objects and seriously constrain the evocation of selves. A limited form of education must inevitably ensue from these conditions.

Being, Object Relations, and the Self

Being, it would seem, is the active establishment of object relations. The self of my twenty-two-month-old daughter is constructed as a product of that activity. Psychotherapist Frank Summers (1994, 346) says, "Any object relations theory leads to a concept of the self, the development of which is linked to the vicissitudes of the object relations units." It is upon these units that psychological structure is built. That infants have this phenomenological existence and that it is the basis for the development of self has been the subject of much recent theory and research. These studies suggest that this development of self is, indeed, situated in the establishment of object relations. The reaching out to the world that is the infant's activity is facilitated by the caregivers; from their responses the child learns a way of being in the world, becomes a self in relation to, and in the use of, objects. Daniel Stern (1985) lists four types of experience that are needed to form a sense of the core self. These are self-agency, self-coherence, self-affectivity, and self-history. Each of these evolves within an environment that may be facilitating. That is, the environment responds to the infant, and these responses affect the structuring of the core self. So an infant who attempts to turn from a face and is not permitted to do so learns something about boundaries and develops a sense of self based on this sense. An infant who is given freedom of movement and exploration builds a sense of agency and expectations. Christopher Bollas writes (1987, 50) that "For each schema from the baby's inherited disposition there is a schema of maternal coverage. The baby and then the child internalizes as structure a process that is a dialectically negotiated composition of his own instincts and ego interests and the mother's handling of them." As a result of early care, the child internalizes rules for being based on its relations to objects. Being becomes the expression of the internalized and unconscious rules learned in an environment that facilitates this learning.

As I will later suggest, it is not sufficient that an object be related to; the object must be made available for use to facilitate expression of self. But before an object can be used (Winnicott, 1971) it must first be related to; the development of the maturational processes, the development of self (to use Winnicott's phrasings), is organized by the relations in which the organism actively engages with objects in the environment in which it is held. These relations become the structure of the psychic self, and the holding environment becomes the container in which the process is facilitated. The totality of object relations forms the psychological structure of the individual. These psychological structures are thought of as "object relations units" (Summers 1994, 346). In this paradigm, the psychological structure of the self is not the tripartite model of id, ego, and superego organized by Freud; rather, this exemplar is replaced by the notion of the self as the totality of object relations. As Summers (346) says, " . . . in object relations theories the importance of ego structure wanes in favor of the development of self structure, which is a product of the internalization of attachments in the form of object relationships . . . The way the self structure is experienced at any given moment is the sense of self; that is, the phenomenological experience of the self, the sense of self, is a reflection of the underlying self structure." The postmodern decentered self is not a fragmented subjectivity but a complex structure that may be expressed in relationships with objects that evoke separate and distinct selves. Subjectivity is the meaningful interpretation of self in experience. Subjectivity is founded in object relations.

Object relations, then, are conceptualized as the cornerstones of development. In his essay "The Use of an Object," Winnicott

(1971, 88) states: "In object relating the subject allows certain alterations in the self to take place, of a kind that has caused us to invent the term cathexis. The object has become meaningful." What has become internalized, however, is not the object per se but the processes by which the infant is the Other's object and in which the Other becomes the child's object. What is internalized is a relationship. Later, what I will refer to as the subject, the experiential and reflectively aware aspect of the person (Bollas 1989, 51) is called into existence as the object of his own unconscious ego processes. The subject is the product of the continuous evocation and reflection upon object use. Daniel Dennett (1992) has described consciousness as the precipitation of a particular narrative upon the stimulus of a particular problem. The production of narrative is made possible and organized by objects that are available and their potential uses. "If you think of yourself as a center of narrative gravity . . . your existence depends on the persistence of that narrative . . . which could *theoretically* survive indefinitely many switches of *medium*, be teleported as readily (in principle) as the evening news, and stored indefinitely as sheer information" (Dennett 1992, 430). Consciousness is an event; it is, as Dewey might say, the meaning of events in the course of their remaking. The subject is the construct of a particular probe that results from a particular interaction with the environment. Reality is always being drafted; reality is always in process. Subjectivity derives from my conscious center of narrative gravity; my subjectivity's representation is a matter of narrative strategies and resources. Narrative gravities and strategies are produced in object relations. The music that sets my daughter swaying and leads her to dancing derives its power from its position as meaningful object; her dancing transforms her into a dancer. The subject is not unitary nor even continuous; rather, the subject becomes the process of addressing the object that is our self and that is evoked in the use of objects. Subjectivity is a position or a stance, and its expression depends on its object relations. Subjectivity is a consequence of a consciousness of the self as object.

The potential availability of objects is, of course, infinite but also contingent. As we mature we have the mobility and enhanced capacity to discover objects and to use them, though again we have limited control over the objects that may at any time be available. And much of the manner of our object relating is steeped in what Bollas (1989, 213-14) calls the unthought known, "knowledge that as yet is not thought." For example, although children often live in family moods or practices that are beyond their comprehension, they nevertheless participate in the actual living of such events and in such knowledge. Much of the environment of infants is facilitated by the primary caregivers.[4] During the earliest moments of a child's existence, the environment in which the infant is held is the whole of human culture and is represented almost entirely by the caregivers and their own "psychic genera" (see Bollas, 1992). These psychic genera may be defined as the dynamic organizing structures of psychic life and are based in the interplay between the natural idiom of the individual and the objects that are available in the environment to that individual. Psychic genera are the organizing structures by which data may be perceived and from which connections may be made. They are the motes of dust about which drops of rain form. Perhaps we might consider psychic genera as originally the unconscious ego's structures based in a necessity for "inner organization, pattern, coherence, the basic need to discover identity in difference without which experience becomes chaos" (Milner 1987, 84). They are the psychic incubators of libidinal cathexes of the object world. Psychic genera seem to be the structures of object relations. Bollas (1992, 47) writes that "All ego attitudes, feelings and operations indicate, even if we cannot grasp it, the trace of an object relation." Psychic genera are the nucleus by which the world might be organized, from which an outlook on life may be derived, and from which new questions and works may be secured. These genera facilitate engagement with the world by promoting contact in it to evoke affective and ideational states that are the self. They are understood as bits of experience (ideas, words, images, experiences, affects) "when experience evokes intense psychic interest" that is internalized and unconscious; these genera then can subsequently "scan the world of experience for phenomena related to such

---

[4] Nancy Chodorow (1978) has shown how this early caregiving is gender based and gender biased.

inner work" (Bollas, 1992). Genera might be considered the object relations units spoken of above. They facilitate the connections that may be made between the internal and the external. For the infant the psychic genera of the caregivers organize not only the objects in the environment but are themselves objects from which the infant's psychic structure may be constructed.

This emphasis on the early holding environment as the origin of character situates the focus of object relations theorists on the preoedipal stage of a child's development when these early object relations are formed. It is from the qualia of these early object relations that will depend the organization and the development of the self. But as Winnicott argues, to talk about childhood, the space of the origin of object relating and of psychic genera, inevitably we must talk about the adolescent and the adult; the establishment of object relations in childhood has a lasting effect on the adult. In his discussion concerning the growth of a sense of guilt from which care and human involvement develop in the individual, Winnicott notes the relationship between the different "stages" of life: he writes (1986, 81) that to talk of the developing sense of guilt in a five-year-old, "we know we are talking about the whole of childhood, particularly about adolescence; and if we're talking about adolescence, we are talking about adults, because no adults are all the time adult. This is because people are not just their own age; they are to some extent every age, or no age." Christopher Bollas (1989, 51) notes that "Our handling of our self as an object partly inherits and expresses the history of our experience as the parental object, so that in each adult it is appropriate to say that certain forms of self perception, self facilitation, self handling and self refusal express the internalized parental process still engaged in the activity of handling the self as object." The uses of the object—including the self as object—derive from early object relations. Our adult object relations contain within them those of the child; although the earliest object relations are formed within the family structure and the good enough environment of the home, it is to the educational apparatus that we must look for the provision of objects by which the self may be evoked and subjectivity derived and for the provision of an environment where objects may be played with safely without fear of either its destruction or its retaliation. Schools are where we might find our children; in adults is where we find our childhood.

Our lives may be said to derive from the uses of objects, and this is ultimately a creative process. How objects are used derives from the effects of a facilitating environment that enables the child to actually find what the child creates, to create and to link up that creation with the Real. "The fact is that what we create is already there, but the creativeness lies in the way we get at perception through conception and apperception," Winnicott writes (1986, 52-53). "What I want to make clear is that creative living involves, in every detail of its experience, a philosophical dilemma—because, in fact, in our sanity we only create what we find." Although objects are already there to be found, their actual use may be indeterminable. An object's identity is founded on its use: the rifles framed on my wall, encased in my hunting cabinet, or cradled in my arms atop an abandoned building bear the same arbitrary name but are very different objects and are used differently. The rifle is a different object when I use its barrel to hammer in a nail that will finally hold it up on the wall. When I use the object differently I evoke a different self. What we find may be always invested with the dream—our wishes and desires—but nonetheless, we can only use an object if it is already there to be used. Just as external objects are used in the service of the sleeping dream, in our waking lives we can use the object according to our wills. We may only find in the world what is already there, but it is the malleability of the object that makes its use possible. The use of the object derives from object relations; object relations offer an explanation of self steeped in the material of the world. As Bollas (1987, 9) says, the person's *self* is the history of many internal relations. The self consists of object relations and is expressed through the uses of the objects.

Object relations theory offers explanations for agency from the first moments of birth; it is clear that during the first moments after birth infants already begin to relate to objects.[5]

---

[5] Moments after her birth, our daughter Anna Rose responded to my singing "Puff, the Magic Dragon." By response I mean an active attention to my face precipitated by my beginning to sing. During the several months

That early relationship derives first from the natural idiom of the neonate. That idiom, says Bollas (1989, 9), is a "genetically biased set of dispositions." Thoreau (1961, 61) speaks of the effects of this idiom when he says "I know of no redeeming qualities in myself but a sincere love for some things, and when I am reproved I fall back on to this ground." This idiom, or "love for some things,"[6] is what Dysart spoke of above concerning Alan Strang's particular passion.

Of course, this idiom is only a potential, for it requires care and objects for its evolution. Its original expression always depends on the caregiver's interpretation and thus occurs only in an environment which facilitates such expression.[7] "The mother's and father's process of care, which demonstrates their own complex conscious and unconscious rules for being and relating, constitutes the facilitating environment and is the matrix which serves as a space for the infant's projections and for his introjections" (Bollas 1987, 60). What Winnicott (1984, 94) refers to as aggression—one of the two main sources of an individual's energy—are the "infantile hittings [that] lead to a discovery of the world that is not the infant's self, and to the beginnings of a relationship to external objects . . . what is aggressive behaviour is therefore at the start a simple impulse that leads to a movement and to the beginnings of explora-

---

preceding her birth, several different versions of "Puff, the Magic Dragon" were played regularly in the house and car by our older daughter, Emma. It was clear to me that Anna Rose arrived in the world already familiar and comfortable with the song. She engaged my face for at least a full minute, observing my face in general and the movements of my mouth specifically. Music has consistently been an active force in both our children's lives and has a particularly calming effect on them.

[6] An aversion to some things, even an obliviousness to some things, may be understood as well as a product of that idiom.

[7] Swaddling is an early form of interpretation and organizes much of the child's original explorations. Lloyd deMause (1974, 11) says that "the belief that infants were felt to be on the verge of turning into totally evil beings is one of the reasons why they were tied up, or swaddled, so long and so tightly." Joseph Illick (1974, 327) writes that though there is no record of swaddling in America "it is clear that American parents were admonished to take a strong stand against self-assertion, or willfulness, in children. Breaking the will of the child was based on the supposition that the parents' will could be substituted."

tion." How this "aggression" is handled, for example, in the facilitating environment will have influence on the development of ego structure. The ego is the unconscious organizing processes that reflect our mental structures; the ego is the internalized rules for being and relating, canons for how to process internal and external reality. It is comprised, as I have said, of object relations. This organization begins first in the holding environment of the primary caregivers, and it is the basis of our psychic life. "The psyche [ego] is that part of us which represents through self and object representations the dialectics of true-self negotiation with the actual world" (Bollas 1989, 9). The ego is perhaps a grammar from which character may be expressed. That representation of character must be made in a process: our character is a process that may be observed in the "person's use of others as objects (transferences) and how he relates to and handles himself as an object (self as object transference and countertransference)" (Bollas 1989, 60). Those inner objects are highly condensed psychic structures that are the trace of our encounters with the object world. It is not the object that is internalized; rather, it is a process derived from an object. There is always more to the object than its physical sense; there is more to the object than its affective presence. The Freudian concepts of condensation, displacement, overdetermination, and secondary elaboration become meaningful in object relations.

Thus it is argued that the primary need of the human being is not for the discharge of drive tension but the development of object relations. It is through object relations that self comes into being. "From the very beginning, babies notice and appreciate people, or, in the language of the laboratory, they prefer social to nonsocial stimuli . . . The features of faces—light and dark contrast, movement, three-dimensionality—are exactly the features that infants prefer in visual discrimination experiments" (Astington 1993, 37). Indeed, within a few days newborns prefer live faces to two-dimensional depictions of faces and can discriminate their parents' faces from those of strangers. Stern's (1985, 42) review of the research, as well as his own developmental studies, shows that "From birth on, there appears to be a central tendency to form and test hypotheses about what is occurring in the world. Infants are also constantly evaluating, in the sense of asking, is this different from or the same as that? How discrepant is what I have just encountered from what I have previously encountered?" This tendency (what Winnicott refers to as aggression) Stern says, will produce a categorization of the world into features that are invariant and those that are variant. The child will begin to develop a sense of self based in its object relations: in its object relating the infant will discover what belongs to her/him and what belongs to the environment. That self will derive from the relationship between the individual idiom and the objects through which that idiom may be expressed. The world must be there to be used, but its use is individual. J. J. Gibson (1979, 7) notes that " . . . in one sense the surroundings of a single animal are the same as the surroundings of all animals but that in another sense the surroundings of a single animal are different from those of any other animal." We can only behave with respect to those objects we can look at or feel, or smell or taste or hear. "The sense organs of animals, the perceptual systems, are not capable of detecting atoms or galaxies." We are expressed (our idioms are expressed) as a result of the objects we use and by the manner in which those objects are used. Irnerio, a character in Italo Calvino's novel *if on a winter's night a traveler* (1979, 149), boasts that he never reads; nevertheless he enters Ludmilla's apartment in pursuit of books: "It's not for reading. It's for making. I make things with books. I make objects. Yes, artworks: statues, pictures, whatever you want to call them . . . A book is a good material to work with; you can make all sorts of things with it." Irnerio is an artist: he boasts that photographs of his artwork will be placed in books that he will then use for new art works.[8] Our selves derive from our relations with and use of objects.

Even the development of language seems to be based on the compulsion to share—to form relations. Neonates are not passive receptors merely reacting to caregivers; rather, newborns by their actions require and shape behaviors in the caregivers. Colwyn Trevarthen (1980, 338) notes that " . . . before they accept a decontextualized representation of a common reality,

---

[8] For a more complete expression of this process see my "Curriculum as Affichiste," forthcoming.

humans direct their will and experience precisely toward learning common enterprises with others and sharing common artifacts. They communicate their wants in relation to what others may do for them. They push the responses of their caretakers toward a shared understanding, and they develop in direct response to the quality and freedom of this understanding." Language is prepared for by a seemingly intrinsic motive to relate, by a desire to seek and find relations. And in that desire for object relating, the neonate shapes the behavior of others and is not a mere passive recipient.

Motives for intersubjectivity, Trevarthen (1980) notes, may be present in some form from birth. Recent study reveals that the fundamental human need is not for the discharge of drives as postulated by Freud but is, rather, for the attainment of object contact. Language is only one means of developing that contact and is not a prerequisite for it. Even when psychoanalysts subscribe to drive theory they do so in the service of object relating. After all, a drive can, it is argued, only be expressed through an object relationship. In this sense, the discharge of drives is not motivated by the relief of biological tension but by the desire for the formation of object relations. "It may be said," psychotherapist Frank Summers reports (1994, 345) "that all object relations theories view the formation of object relations as the primary human motivation." This, indeed, is what Trevarthen's research suggests. Although motives may reflect experience and may become more specialized through learning, they appear also to be a schema for the perception of the "affordances" of an object.[9] One such motive for object relating may be hypothesized as the motive (Trevarthen 1980, 327):

> To respond with such expressions of pleasure, then with manifestations of special human expression such as gestures and utterances, these being coordinated from the start with concurrent or intervening interests toward impersonal surroundings and objects that might be commented on or used cooperatively. Some forms of expression are clearly preadaptive to the later acquisition of cultivated forms of communication, including a true language. Most important of these

---

[9] Affordances have been defined by Gibson as the things about an object that do not change.

are prespeech movements of lips and tongue, cooing vocalizations
associated with prespeech, and gestures of the hands. These signs of
expressive motivation lack mental representations of conventional
topics.

Language, then, rather than facilitating object relations actually can be theorized to derive from those relations.

Furthermore, recent research (Stern 1985) confirms what
Bollas notes about the structures of psychological development.
This work suggests that neonates organize the self based on
relationships to objects. Stern (1985, 10) writes:

> [Infants] are predesigned to be selectively responsive to external so-
> cial events and never experience an autistic-like phase . . . during the
> period from two to six months, infants consolidate the sense of a core
> self as a separate, cohesive, bounded, physical unit, with a sense of
> their own agency, affectivity, and continuity in time . . . the period of
> life from roughly nine to eighteen months is not primarily devoted to
> the developmental tasks of independence or autonomy or individua-
> tion—that is, of getting away and free from the primary caregiver. It is
> equally devoted to the seeking and creating of intersubjective union
> with another . . .

It would appear that wired into infants is the desire to interact,
to gain information from others, and to share things: to engage in object relations. Colwyn Trevarthen (1980, 324) says,
"The totality of the baby's rudimentary powers to use external
objects to satisfy perception, exploration, manual prehension
and the like I call *subjectivity*—the condition of being a coordi-
nated subject, motivated to act with purpose in relation to the
world outside."

Different theorists might posit a different basis for these
object relations. For example, whereas for Melanie Klein the
vicissitudes of aggression and its integration with good objects
are the critical components of self formation, for Winnicott it
is the availability of the "environmental mother" who can provide background support for the natural unfolding of the self,
which process facilitates the internalization of the good enough
mother which permits the maturational process to unfold.
Object relations theorists differ about the function of the object in the psychic structure, but all object relations theorists
seem to agree that psychic structure is built on the process of
object relating and that the self is evoked in object use. "While
one cannot justifiably speak of a single object relations theory,

each theoretical viewpoint is based on the general principle that autonomously motivated attachments to early figures become internalized and form the building blocks of self" (Summers 1994, 350). Nor is it a passive imprint of the relationship that is internalized; rather, what is internalized is the particular manner in which an infant/child construes the relationship (with the original caregivers) and in a specific environment.[10] I think that this process is based in the particular idiom of the infant and the particular defensive and adaptational needs of the infant as a result of the environment. Erikson ([1950] 1993, 95) has noted that

> man's [sic] "inborn" instincts are drive fragments to be assembled, given meaning, and organized during a prolonged childhood by methods of child training and schooling which vary from culture to culture and are determined by tradition . . . man survives only where traditional child training provides him with a conscience which will guide him without crushing him and which is firm and flexible enough to fit the vicissitudes of his historical era.

The particular uses of the object evoke specific forms of self. For example, Shirley Brice Heath (1982) has shown that the relation to an object—language—and its particular uses produce a particular literate self.

If we come to being in object relations and if our selves are evoked in object use, then to be a character—indeed, to know a character—requires that we recognize how it is that an object evokes a particular self and to know the history of our selves and the object relations upon which our selves are based. In our conscious and unconscious use of objects we "imagine ourselves" into being. We become, as it were, the dream work of our own lives.

---

[10] To risk a gender ticket (a phrase I gain from my dear friend, William Pinar) I must say that the role of the father as a caregiver has been undertheorized in the psychological literature I have studied. I believe that there is a rich field for harvest in the study of the good enough father and his role in providing the good enough environment for the unfolding of the maturational processes. Admittedly, Winnicott's theorizing took place in a world of clear and distinct gender roles; however, the critical changes that took place starting in at least the 1950s in familial relations based in gender and the increasingly difficult economic situation in the United States require a rethinking of the role of parental caregiving.

> When we use an object it is as if we know the terms of engagement; we
> know we shall "enter into" an intermediate space, and at this point of
> entry we change the nature of perception, as we are now released to
> dream work, in which subjectivity is scattered and disseminated into
> the object world, transformed by that encounter, then returned to it-
> self after the dialectic, changed in its inner contents by the history of
> that moment (Bollas 1992, 60).

As our unconscious ego processes are released into objects
chosen for the dream to evoke a dreaming self by object choice,
and as those objects are changed in the encounter, so too in
the waking dream might we choose our objects based on unconscious ego processes and object relations so that a self is
evoked. From that encounter, subjectivity may develop. I would
that curriculum be understood in this fashion; then what an
education that would be!

We can often identify objects that can call us into a "dreaming episode" when we could elaborate the self; it is only by
reflection that we do in the dream. That is, we might understand an evoked self by consideration of the objects in the
dream. How the dream is constructed might give insight into
the evocation of character. And it is to the possibility of dreaming—to the environment that facilitates the dream—that we
might look to offer us insight into the role education might
play in the evocations and developments of self. It is to the
dream that we might look for the exemplar of self-evocation in
the use of objects even as the use of the dream itself as object
might give us some insight into subjectivity and creativity.

"Dreams," says Thoreau (1961, 370), "are the touchstones of
our characters. We are scarcely less afflicted when we remember some unworthiness in our conduct in dream, than if it had
been actual." Contemporary dream theory offers support for
Thoreau's intuitive belief in dreams: the reality of dreams offers insight into character. If being derives from object relations, then perhaps we must look at the being in dreams as
deriving similarly; for in dreams objects are used for an evocation of a self by an unconscious idiom seeking expression. We
must look at dreams as expressive of object relations even as
they may be understood as objects themselves. I would like to
pursue the analogy between waking and dreaming to see if
education might be informed by this confluence. As the world

of waking life may partake of the world of the dream, perhaps education as an exemplar of the waking life might be informed by the insights dreams offer us about the lives of children. For if, as Thoreau suggests, we can be most truthful in dreams, then we must look to dreams as an authentic place for experiencing self and constructing subjectivity. Then we might understand how to facilitate such efforts of experiencing and constructing in waking life. I would like to pursue the reality of dreams and the dreamlike reality of waking life.

Chapter III

The Stuff of Dreams

Such Stuff as Dreams are Made On

Seated at the play he has constructed for what he hopes is the pleasure and edification of Miranda and Ferdinand, his daughter and future son-in-law, Prospero, the magician in Shakespeare's *The Tempest*, responds to a concern expressed by his children.[1] Despite the delight they experience from the staged pageant, they see perturbation upon his wizened face and are perhaps concerned that the pageant he has produced for them is causing him discomfort and alarm. They ask, perhaps, for assurance that the play is not real, that it is all comprised of spirits and other ephemera, that the pageant is merely the construction of Prospero's mind and ought not have material substance enough to disturb Prospero. They want guarantee, in fact, that they have not misperceived the pageant. Although delighted at its presentation, they are troubled by Prospero's change in mood, and they wonder at its cause.

In fact, Prospero's agitation results not at all from the events in his pageant but from his consideration of the imminent arrival of those who would plot against him and of the necessity to deal with these unpleasant people and in a manner most unpleasant. He is thinking, in fact, about another pageant, one that does not yet exist but one that he is yet constructing; the self evoked is a product of object relations reflectively known

---

[1] In actuality Ferdinand is not Prospero's child but (a) Prospero has led Ferdinand to believe his own father has drowned and he, thus, assumes the surrogate role of parent; and (b) throughout the play Ferdinand is educated to be Miranda's husband and, thus, Prospero's child by law.

only to Prospero. And so Prospero reassures his children that his distress does not derive from the reality of the play because, as he suggests, it contains no reality *until it is invested with one—* as we do in and with dreams. Indeed, as we the audience know, Prospero was not even paying attention.

Life itself obtains, Prospero suggests, from the same relations between world and self as do dreams; neither can be externally scripted for subsequent interpretation. Like the play, Prospero avers, life itself partakes of no immutable or incontrovertible reality. The play is, as is a dream and as is life, a construction, inhabited by "Spirits, which by mine art/I have from their confines call'd to enact/My present fancies" (IV,i,120-22). Prospero suggests that our lives are a dream; like the pageant, dreams and life may be fleeting, but they do not lack meaning. Rather, meaning must be made from them and is not implicit in them. So too will be the origin of the next pageant—his present fancies—the one he is now contemplating. Antedating Sigmund Freud by several hundred years but without his technical vocabulary, Prospero avers that the nature of a person's character ("my present fancies") may be evoked in the operations of the dream work in waking life. Life is but a dream. He comforts his children (IV, i, 148-58):

> These our actors
> As I foretold you, were all spirits and
> Are melted into air, into thin air;
> And, like the baseless fabric of this vision,
> The cloud-capp'd towers, the gorgeous palaces,
> The solemn temples, the great globe itself,
> Yea, all which it inherit, shall dissolve,
> And like this insubstantial pageant faded,
> Leave not a rack behind. We are such stuff
> As dreams are made on, and our little life
> Is rounded with a sleep.

Now, I do not think that in these lines Prospero has in mind the radical idealism that will culminate in George Berkeley's seeming dismissal of physical reality in the eighteenth century. Although Prospero avers that our lives are a dream, I do not think he means that they are wholly generated as the independent product of mind and are completely ephemeral and transitory. Dreams, Shakespeare knew, are more significant than that. The physical world is not wholly the product of the subjective; the physical world is not the product of the projective realization of the dream. Prospero does not invent Ariel, but he does by his magic control him and will ultimately set him free. Objects may be used, but they must also be available for use. In *The Tempest* the physical world is there and available to perception and use by those creative enough to do so. In the drama the meaning of perception is not in the act of perceiving—of seeing the spirits—but in the idea of the construction of the percept, of knowing to look for spirits and finding them. Prospero's magic enables him to make of the spirits what he would; the same is not true for any other character in the play. Ferdinand and Miranda see the same spirits as Prospero, but they respond differently to their perception: they distinguish between material and spiritual. They are concerned about what they see; they would understand what they see but they do not understand that meaning derives from their own construction. They ask Prospero what is meant by the play. If these are only spirits and not material, Ferdinand wonders, they must have no meaning. I think he would be willing to understand Prospero's words to mean that like the pageant, we are such stuff as dreams: impermanent and inconsequential, perhaps even a bit unreal. Ferdinand has a lot to learn. But Prospero does not say we are dreams; rather, he says we are the stuff that dreams are made on. And if we are such stuff as dreams are made on, Prospero might mean that our lives have the same structure and meaning as dreams and not necessarily that dreams are unreal.

And I do not think that Prospero suggests in these lines that his life is but a dream constructed solely in the mind from perceptions; after all, in *The Tempest* Prospero's enemies have been real and dangerous and have caused him to suffer grave physical threat even though he had originally been unaware of those enemies. Whether he perceived them or not, they existed. How it was that he was incapable of seeing the dangers before him he acknowledges as his blindnesses and therefore part of his knowledge. Indeed, as Duncan acknowledged in *Macbeth*, "There's no art to find the mind's construction in the face." Perception is not the beginning of knowledge. Certainly, Prospero must have read of such corrupt activity in the studies in which he engaged and that, it is said, led to his ill-fated neglect of the material world. Furthermore, were the world wholly of his own making and deriving from his own perception, why would Prospero have invented the evil that exiled both him and his daughter? Gerald Edelman (1992, 35) maintains that Berkeley's monistic idealism is an inadequate explanation for the substance of consciousness: it is incompatible at least with the very idea of evolution, the theory upon which Edelman's idea of mind and consciousness is founded. "It would be very strange indeed if we mentally created an environment that then subjected us (mentally) to natural selection." No, the dream of which Prospero speaks must partake of a real object world, albeit one in which his relations have organized specific uses of objects that might evoke specific selves. Ariel as object plays many roles in *The Tempest,* all of which are ordered by Prospero, who constructs his days by his use of the available objects.

Nor do I believe that Prospero's belief in the dreamlike reality of existence argues for a political withdrawal into a spiritual cocoon. This was Descartes' error: that he was all alone in his room and he was capable of thinking himself into existence. In fact, however, just such a retreat had led earlier to Prospero's overthrow by his seditious brother, Sebastian; indeed, I think Prospero's ultimate acknowledgment of the reality of the physical world and his necessary place in its materiality comes with his recognition of his relationship to Caliban.[2] Prospero, too, has been a student in *The Tempest.* Furthermore, this withdrawal from the world, referred to in the latter part of the twentieth century as the retreat into narcissism, is often attributed to the belief that the ego can only achieve growth when it is removed from the world's demands for conformity. We may think ourselves into reality; the quest for self-actualization or self-realization then, suggests that the world can be dismissed to achieve a reality of the self. The social world is discarded to give birth to the self-actualized individual entity. This belief, too, maintains the Cartesian split between mind and body, inner and outer worlds that I do not believe are con-

---

[2] " . . . this thing of darkness I/Acknowledge mine," Prospero admits of Caliban. For a wonderful discussion of the blackness of whiteness see Pinar (1991) and Morrison (1994).

tained in the idea of Prospero's dream. "Critics of the Awareness Movement are correct in arguing that considering intricacy as 'only inner' hides the social controls that make it seem *only* inner" (Gendlin 1987, 258). Human complexity exists, but not separate from the world in which that complexity may come to form. No, Prospero's dream does not speak of an existence isolated from the real world—as in fantasy—composed of images existing solely in the mind.

Rather, in these oft-quoted lines I think that Prospero, the good magician, points to the twentieth-century advocacy that we and the world we inhabit derive from our construction of it and in which construction perception is a willed, not an originary, act. I have suggested that the materials of that construction are object relations units. The materials for that constructivist process lie in the objects that are available to us and our possible creative use of those objects. I think Prospero means, indeed, that our lives are a waking dream. Or as Thoreau (1961, 371) says, "Our truest life is when we are in dreams awake." I would like to suggest that in our dreams we elaborate and experience our selves. The uses of the dream—what Ferdinand and Miranda must learn—are the practices of education and must be facilitated. Let me pursue this. If we elaborate the dream perhaps we might understand the potentialities for education.

Dream a Little Dream of Me

I do not know precisely about what my twenty-two-month-old daughter dreams. Without adult language she cannot tell me. I do not doubt, however, that she dreams nor that her dreams derive from her active phenomenological life. I do not doubt that it is she who dreams. During her sleep she vocalizes, she whimpers and coos, she moves about forcefully and in ways to which I attribute volition. Sometimes she awakens agitatedly from this activity. I walk the floors with her. My six-year-old daughter also dreams, and she too, vocalizes, utters English words I recognize, whimpers, and moves forcefully about. Sometimes during these sleep-enactments she even impels herself out of bed. I pick her up and place her back into a calmer sleep. If she awakens, she may tell me her dreams, but more often than not she falls immediately back to sleep and in the morning there is no dream. Clearly, there is more to their sleep than rest. But what? I do not doubt that it is she who dreams. I understand that it is she immersed in experience in the dream—who else could it be?—and that that experience reflects her diurnal life. What else is there? I do not doubt that it is she who dreams.

I interpret my daughters' behavior; I teach them to think about their own behavior. But there must first be self immersed in experience in the dream and in life for me or for them to think about. I want now to ponder upon the daughters immersed in the dream. I have used the personal pronouns "she" and "her" to refer to my daughters' dreaming selves but I wonder about whom I am speaking. Who in the dreams are my daughters?

I think that their experience in the dream—their selves in the dream—derive from their object relations and use. My daughters' dreams are the experiencing of selves using objects that derive from their waking, phenomenal lives. That is, using objects from her waking world the dream is constructed and a self is evoked. Tonight in one daughter's dreams plays "Puff, the Magic Dragon"; tomorrow night perhaps a different music will appear. The self evoked in the dream is elicited by the objects chosen by the idiom to express itself. Perhaps tomorrow as part of the sound track of the day "Puff, the Magic Dragon" will play. She will ask that we play it in the car on the way to school. It will provide a color to her day as a particular evocation of self is accomplished.

Of course, there is no single unitary self that produces the dream, no homunculus directing consciousness. Rather, as I have suggested, that self is comprised of object relations units and is a potentiality evoked by the impingement of an environment. The dream is produced from those relations—it is a draft of reality (see above) that derives from unconscious ego processes. But the self evoked is so evoked by the elected objects of the dream. Dream life, Freud acknowledges, is the way our mind works during sleep and when its stimuli are all self-generated. But I am concerned with the idea of "mind," which is comprised as I have suggested of object relations units. I am concerned equally with the pronoun "our." For whatever mind may be, it must be ours to have; I would suggest that the dream creates the particular self that is immersed in the experience of the dream. Since the individual is not a unitary subject but rather an incredibly complex self, our dreams derive from the unconscious ego processes expressing their idiom through the objects available to it in the lexicon of objects. "Our" in this sense is the potential self actualized in the objects of the dream. In the language of object relations theory then, the dreaming self and the dream script in which it acts derive from early object relations and are comprised of the lexicon of objects that have been psychically charged and that have been nominated to evoke different aspects of the self which is always only a potentiality. The dream (re)presents the self in experience. Dream a little dream of me.

Throughout much of the time, we are in the dream what Bollas (1992) refers to as simple selves. That is, we are unreflective and experiencing selves simply moving about in the dream amidst the various objects that the ego has nominated; we are actors "alive in a theater of represented parts." Within the dream this unreflective self endures deep experiences in this arena. The simple self is not, however, aware that it is a self walking about in the theater of its represented parts. In the dream "the Dreamer is present in experience but absent in knowledge" (Phillips 1993, 65). Rather, the simple self simply experiences. Its experiences in the dream are the product of the ego, "the unconscious organizing process—the logic of operations—[whose] choices will ultimately reflect both the innate true self (an organization that is its precursor) and the subsequent structures developed out of partnership with the mother and father," and by extension, the rest of the world of objects and experiences (Bollas 1989, 17). In the dream, the self experiences; in the dream the self that might later be used as an object is evoked by the objects in the dream. In this case the dream would show to those who could see it the self engaged in experience in the theater of its represented parts. That dream may be interpreted, but the experience of the dream is available only to the self evoked in it. The dream is where the self is evoked in its engagement with objects, events, selves, and persons elected because they have been psychically charged within the environment. In the dream the dreamer has visions of "the self in transformed states that are nonetheless articulations of the individual's unique person" (Bollas 1989, 47). Dream a little dream of me.

The dream represents an activity of play. I think that within the safety of the dream we permit ourselves to become *unintegrated*, "scattered islands of organized potentials coming into being" (Bollas 1992, 14-15). The dream is one place—waking life is another—where this potential self may be expressed along with its wishes, desires, anxieties, defenses, and needs. If consciousness may be understood as a particular probe of the narrative stream (see Dennett 1992), a probe resulting from any impingement, then the dream is the evocation of a consciousness by the subject. I will argue along with Dennett that the significance of the dream resides in its audience and that it is the latter that provides the dream's content. Subjectivity is the production of an audience for the dream. What the audience must learn to recognize, of course, is its self. The dream, however, is an expression of a self that achieves evocation through the dream work; the experience of the simple self in the dream is not recoverable. The dreaming self is only a potential actualized in the use of objects itself founded in early object relations, early caregivers. The dream is the place where the rules of being which derive from object relations in the early environment function; the early interpretations of the caregivers become the unthought known of the infant. Bollas (1992, 14) says that to be in a dream is

> a continuous reminiscence of being inside the maternal world where one was partly a receptive figure within a comprehending environment. Indeed, the productive intentionality that determines the dream we are in and that never reveals itself (i.e. "where is the dreamer that dreams the dream?") uncannily recreates, in my view, the infant's relation to the mother's unconscious, which although it does not show itself nonetheless produces the process of maternal care. In this respect the dream seems to be a structural memory of the infant's unconscious, an object relation of person inside the other's unconscious processing.

If dreams are the place where "unintegration" might be experienced, then it is in dreams that the self may experience the least resistance for its expression. Winnicott (1965, 34) defines "unintegration" as " a state in which there is no orientation, to be able to exist for a time without being either a reactor to an external impingement or an active person with a direction of interest or movement." From this stage of unintegration an impulse will arrive leading to direction. Adam Phillips (1993, 74) notes, for example, that boredom might be considered a waiting for something without knowing what that something might be: "The bored child, a sprawl of absent possibilities, is looking for something to hold his attention." The precipitation of a dream might derive from a type of boredom— a waiting. In this sense, we might understand nightmares as deriving from the fear of separation, of being alone in the dark, of being bored. Similarly, nightmares might originate from the fear of the unintegrated state. Nightmares might derive from object relations. John Mack (1992, 344) says that "many children and adults struggle against the act of falling asleep, as if this helpless surrender were itself dangerous, apart from the anxieties that may be encountered during sleep. The danger associated with relinquishing reality and withdrawing from the outside world, especially from love objects, also contributes to this fear of surrendering to sleep." The dream indeed, even the nightmare, seems an evocation of object relations. In it the unintegrated self might engage in experience. Dream a little dream of me.

In other words, in sleep the energy that holds the self together in the deceptive unitary subjectivity of waking life is dissipated and a form of what could be called madness results. Freud posits that dreams are a result of the sleep state. "The state of sleep," he notes, "involves a turning away from the real external world, and there [away from the real external world] we have the necessary condition for the development of psychosis" (Freud 1992, 39). This does not mean however that the dream is "unreal." Rather, by psychosis I believe that Freud refers not to an actual mental illness but to a phenomenological condition dominated by illusion or, as Bollas would characterize it, by hallucination.

As I have above suggested, we start life with a basic idiom. Again, this idiom is partly inherited and partly a product of the interactions between the inherited inclinations and the environment. This idiom can, of course, only be theorized, but its existence is understood in the experience of parents who have twins unalike or who marvel even at birth at the different personalities of siblings. That *idiom* (Bollas 1989, 9) might be understood as "a set of unique person possibilities specific to this individual and subject in its articulation to the nature of lived experience in the actual world." Perhaps this idiom is the essence of which phenomenologists speak; I prefer to understand it as deriving even from fetal object relations. Infants in the womb, for example, respond differently to Mozart than to Beethoven. Nonetheless, we are all born with a set of unique person possibilities. I believe it is of this idiom that the psychiatrist Martin Dysart in *Equus* speaks when he refers to the forged and shackling chains that snap together seemingly by chance. When my daughters produce their dreams in which they are principal actors brimming with the objects chosen to elaborate their idiom, they express and maintain the psychological structures from which their subjectivities may be expressed. But immersed in the dream, they do not recognize themselves. The dream is an expression of the unthought known. Inside the dream, Bollas (1992, 15) writes, the self "unbeknownst to himself is alive in a theater of his represented parts. But this ignorance allows for the very intriguing rendezvous that takes place as the simple self literally inhabits his unconscious." And if it is true that in waking life an infant is capable of "the same kind of active regulatory traffic with the external world as does anyone at any age" (Stern 1985, 233), then it might be argued that the dreams of the infant serve a similar regulatory functioning. What is regulated is the relations to objects from which relations derive senses of self. Within the dream, moving about in objects produced from the lexicon of objects cathected by the individual idiom of the self, the simple self (Bollas' terminology) engages in profound experiences. Thoroughly engrossed in the subjective, the self is capable of authentic experience. As my daughters play about amongst the objects of the world they, too, are immersed wholly in the subjective, moving about amidst objects they have chosen from their lexicon of objects. In that choice, selves are produced; what is experienced are various manifestations of self evoked from the object encounters that occur in the dream and based on the wishes, desires, fears, etc., of the individual. When my daughters dream, they engage in the use of objects, which use is founded on relations. In that use their selves are evoked. When my daughters dream, they express their idioms through the object choices of the dream. When my daughters dream, they dream themselves into existence. Dream a little dream of me.

In dreams infants too evoke their selves using the lexicon of objects that comprise the psychic structures. That lexicon derives from the cathected objects of our world. Stolorow and Atwood (1992, 281-82) argue that the function of dreams is "to act as the *guardians of psychological structure*, a task dreams accomplish by means of concrete symbolization . . . the images in the dream serve directly to restore or sustain the structural integrity and stability of a subjective world menaced with disintegration." The overdetermined symbol is an object that the ego chooses to evoke the self. In this way the dream organizes the chaos of the unintegrated self and "lifts the self" into view by the subject. Those objects are chosen from the day's residues as means of evoking aspects of the self. The choice of objects and the scripts in which they partake are constructions of the ego and facilitate the self's experience. In other words, the dream seems to operate by an intelligence of object relations and use. The objects of the dream permit the self to be evoked: "We dream . . . select objects before we know why and even then knowing so little" (Bollas 1992, 51). It is for this reason that Bollas describes the dream as (1992, 14) " an intelligence of form that holds, moves, stimulates, and shapes us." In the dream, as in life, my daughters unbeknownst to themselves walk about in a world both familiar and strange, familiar in that the objects are known to them and have been unconsciously chosen to evoke the aspects of self, yet strange because these objects are being used to represent parts of which they remain unaware. The dream is the "origin of vision" where my daughters "play with objects, moving through potential patterns, setting up fields of imagined persons, places, selves and events" (Bollas 1989, 47). And since all activity derives from our use of the object—itself a development of object relations— then as Khan (1974, 294) states, "the self is as much created by its symbols, as it is represented and expressed by them." In our dreams we are called into being by our uses of the object; in our dream the simple self exists in a world of objects that it can use to evoke itself. Dream a little dream of me.

Although in life we may be evoked by objects contingently available, in the dream our control over the objects is relatively complete. Our use of objects nonetheless is learned in the facilitating environment. That diurnal experience depends first on object relations and next on object availability and use. If the self is only a potentiality, then it comes to actualization in objects. How objects become meaningful is situated, Bollas asserts, in the dialectic between one's personal idiom and the world that is actually available. The means of using objects are organized, as I have said above, into psychic genera. Psychic genera (Bollas 1992) are the complement of repressed ideas: whereas the latter constellate in the unconscious and contain experience organized by the constellation, the psychic genera (ideas, words, images, experiences, affects, etc.) constellate into mental areas and actively seek out experience to nourish these constellations. These genera are the dynamic design of an evolving psychic structure based in the child's idiom, which is partly inherited and partly derived from the objects that are made available in the environment and the relations that are enabled there. The notion of character, of personality, comes into being from this interaction. "Each inherited disposition meets up with the actual world and one of the outcomes of this dialectic between personality idiom and human culture is psychic life" (Bollas 1989, 9). This inherited disposition Bollas (1989) refers to as the person's idiom: "Human idiom is that peculiarity of person(ality) that finds its own being through the particular selection and use of the object. In this restricted sense, to be and to appropriate are one." We are what we make of the objects available to us; we are such stuff as dreams are made on. Dream a little dream of me.

Life Is But a Dream

We all walk about in environments of objects some of which we have chosen to evoke us and others that evoke us in their contingency. Psychotherapist Christopher Bollas (1992, 4) says that "we oscillate between thinking ourself out through the selection of objects that promote inner experience and being thought out, so to speak, by the environment which plays upon the self." In this sense, life and dreams might be understood as constructions based in the objects in the world we have invested with a certain significance. We choose an author because we have liked her previous work; we happen upon an author with whom we wish in the future to spend more time.[3] I go to the clothes store to find a shirt and try on several before choosing one to purchase. The shirt I choose is "me" but it does not make me so; rather, it derives from the interaction between my desires and the object's availability. How also to explain entering a store with the desire to buy and exiting the store having purchased nothing? I order clothes from a catalog because the model looks wonderfully attired as would I wish myself to be. "Do we not all live in a world of objects?" asks Bollas (1992, 26). "Do we know anyone who does not?" When I run on the road I am a runner, but when I commute my children to their various summer activities on that same road I am not a runner and the road is different. It evokes different selves. I am different. The world is there to be used, but it must first be available for use. It is this use of objects that constructs the world and our selves. "[W]e use objects," Bollas (1992, 13) tells us, "to initially place and then later to evoke the self . . . the human subject *becomes the dream work of his own life*." In the dream, as I have suggested, the unconscious ego processes—the human idiom—use the day's residues to evoke self. The realities we acknowledge as the self and the world must be understood as our constructions of reality—but they are reality nonetheless. Our idioms are expressed not in the perception of objects but in their use.

If, as I have shown, our psychic structure is built upon object relations, then our waking lives and the characters we become, *as in the dream,* derive from those relations; in object use I become character.[4] "Being a character," says Christopher Bollas (1992, 62), referring to the expression of daily subjectivity, "means bringing along with one's articulating idiom those inner presences—or spirits—that we all contain, now and then

---

[3] I am reminded of Holden Caulfield's standard for a good author: one whom you wish were your friend so that you could call her up after finishing the book to talk further.

[4] I intentionally leave out the article to avoid confusion with the vernacular use of the word "character," which usually refers to an eccentricity.

transferring them to a receptive place in the other, who may knowingly or unknowingly be inhabited by them." I may treat my lovers as mother but they would not necessarily know it; I enjoy my friends for whom the aggressiveness of my conversation is an invitation to engagement. I reread *Hamlet* because I was told I was not capable of reading it at school, reinforcing, perhaps, the inadequacies I learned at home. In other words, as in the dream so too in life do we consecrate the world, so to speak, with our subjectivity; we choose objects that speak us, that bear our imprint even when we may not be fully aware of that imprint. Often indeed, as in habit or superstition or fetishes, objects may have meaning although they have lost their significance.

And the process by which we invest objects in the world with our subjectivity and as objects in the world call out our subjectivity seems to be equivalent to the process by which the self is evoked in dreams. As we are characters in our dream, so too, Bollas (1992, 19) says, do "We live our life in our own private dreaming." We move through the world nominating persons, objects, and events as psychically significant. We give meaning to objects. Objects call us into meaning. In the vast complex world of daily life, I perceive specific objects and do not perceive others, read one book rather than another, listen to Bob Dylan rather than Beethoven, Beethoven rather than the Beatles. I call one particular friend on the telephone in an attempt to express myself or to evoke aspects of my self. I feel like eating pizza rather than chopped steak, soup rather than salad. Often we follow our desires: Thoreau (1980, 105) says that taking a walk began with uncertainty as to direction but always seemed to coincide with a certain idiom: "When I go out of the house for a walk, uncertain as yet whither I will bend my steps, and submit myself to my instinct to decide for me, I find, strange and whimsical as it may seem, that I finally and inevitably settle southwest, toward some particular wood or meadow or deserted pasture or hill in that direction." Indeed, perhaps when we live by our own desires we naturally choose objects that allow us to be immersed in experience. Later this experience may be available for using and knowing but first there must be the subjective self involved wholly in experience. We must be open to that experience. To be wholly involved in experience precludes reflection upon it. Thus Thoreau, committed to journal keeping, admits that "It is not easy to write in a journal what interests us at any time, because to write it is not what interests us"(1961, 415). That experience is occasioned in our object world. "Certain objects, like psychic 'keys,' open doors to unconsciously intense—and rich—experience in which we articulate the self that we are through the elaborating character of our response. This selection constitutes the *jouissance* of the true self, a bliss released through the finding of specific objects that free idiom to its articulation"(Bollas 1992, 17). As in the dream so too in waking life the self engages in experience occasioned by the unconscious ego processes in concert with the available environment. Isn't it our quest to create that life that releases our idiom? Might we not admit with Thoreau that the mass of men live lives of quiet desperation because they are denied the freedom to pursue their desire and may not play? "Let us not, my friends, be wheedled and cheated into good behavior to earn the salt of our eternal porridge, whoever they are that attempt it" (Thoreau 1961, 479.) No, not work but play is essential to realize our desire. In play we may live by our desire and choose objects that free our idiom. "Yet, after all, the truly efficient laborer will not crowd his day with work, but will saunter to his task by a wide halo of ease and leisure, and then do but what he loves best" (Thoreau 1961, 128). Were we to build curriculum on this premise, wouldn't we enable education to a degree unimagined in our contemporary world? Life is but a dream.

Chapter IV

Staging the Dream Asleep and Awake

My daughters' selves derive from their object relations, and as their dreams are organized by those object relations so too are their waking lives founded upon those relations. In their dreams as in life their idiom is expressed in and through object choice. In this activity their selves are evoked. There is no doubt that they actively dream. Upon arising in the morning, or awaking from one of her nightmares, the elder can sometimes even verbalize these sleep enactments. She may even name a manifest content of her dream; she creates narrative but is not conscious of her construction of it. Neither of my daughters can attribute cause to her dreams, which is to say that neither is aware that it is she who produces the dream nor that the events and objects in the dream are objects that have been charged with significance by her and, therefore, have been actively chosen for the dream. She has not yet learned how *to use* the dream as object. Neither do her days take on symbolic status because she is for the most part wholly immersed in experience and not reflective upon it. Occasionally she will note self-states and announce a subjectivity, that she is shy, for example: these are evidence of the beginnings of reflexivity. Nor is my daughter reflectively aware (or if she is, she does not communicate that awareness) that what she dreams will change the world in which she lives, for the objects in the dream will derive energy in the external world from their very existence in the dream even as their presence in the dream derives from her having invested psychic energy in the objects. Outside of her awareness, however, her world may be altered by her dreams. At present she does not consciously learn from her dreams; rather she engages in experience in the dream and beyond her ken she is changed.

Now, I too dream and I know *because I have learned it* that it is I who construct the dream, that the dream stuffs derive from my object relations, and that I may interrogate the dream to discover its objects, its structures, and its functions. I (who observe the dreamer in the dream) may relate to the dream itself as an object; I learn how the dreamer—myself—is managed in the dream, the manifest content, or the particular engagement with objects and experiences; and how the dream itself may be managed by the reflective self whose subjectivity is slightly withdrawn. Then the dream may be used as an object. In this use I uncover object relations; I may construct myself. I discover that "I am inhabited . . . by inner structures that can be felt whenever their name is evoked, and in turn, I am also filled with the ghosts of others who have affected me . . . these 'internal objects' [are] *highly condensed psychic textures*, the trace of our encounters with the object world" (Bollas 1992, 59). It is on the basis of these object relations that the dream is constructed. "In the dream experience," Bollas (1987, 51) notes, "the experiential subject is 'confronted' by the ego's processing of the day's events and by the instinctual and historical associations evoked by the day's events . . . When the dreaming subject lives amidst the dream event, the person encounters that oddity of human existence: the subject is face to face with the process of being and relating that constitutes his psychic structure." The furniture, events, and objects in the dream are invested with significance not only because they are in the dream but become highly charged in waking life as well because of their presence in the dream. This capacity to use the dream—to play not only in the dream but with the dream—depends on the ability to realize the dream space. This notion of space is a conscious construction.

We might understand the dream as a biological necessity, but it is in the conscious creation of the dream space where the significance of the dream might be situated.[1] It is in that

---

[1] Dreaming, it would seem, can only be repressed medically. Dreaming seems to be at least a biological activity. And biologically the dream seems to occur without our will; its function biologically may be to preserve psychic and physical health. "We may well have to add to Freud's dictum that

space that the dream is recognized—indeed, is constructed—as an object by the dreamer. This dream space may be understood as a transitional space (Khan, 1974) or the transitional object (Winnicott, 1971; Bollas, 1992) where the self may be evoked in object use. In the dream, unconscious ego processes choose objects in a series to represent aspects of self. In the selection of objects, we transform our inner experience by bringing forth psychic textures (elicited through objects in a series) that bring us into differing areas of potential being. This is true of waking and dreaming life, and perhaps the schizophrenic's terror at the loss of self leads her to choose objects uneconomically in both waking and sleeping life. We are subjects in our dreams moving about in objects of our choosing. The self experiences in the dream: the dream itself might also be available to knowledge.

For the dream to be available, there must exist the notion of space. In the dream space the dream is recognized as an object, and aspects of self evoked in the dream may be known. For the realization of this space, the dream must be placed outside omnipotent control (it must survive our destruction of it) and be known as an external phenomenon and not merely as a projective entity. We may be such stuff as dreams are made on, but indeed, we are stuff. In this construction we might acknowledge a self that stands outside experience in the dream and observes and evaluates and interprets—plays *with* the dream rather than *in* it. That is, there must be the self who has knowledge *of* the dream rather than experience *in* it. Similarly, we

---

the dream is the guardian of sleep, that sleep is necessary in order to safeguard our need to dream" (Greenson 1992, 85). It has also been argued (Fisher 1992, 438) that "REM sleep and its associated dreaming were necessary psychobiological processes, that variations, deficits or excesses of this organismic state could be correlated with mental disorders and that severe and prolonged suppression would produce psychosis in man [sic]." Although some research suggests that this may not be the case, Fisher (1992) found that the suppression of dreams led not to compensatory increases in dreamlike activity, but rather that the cognitive processes that function during waking and that are also responsible for the formation of dreams are disrupted. It may be that we can function fairly well without dreaming, but we cannot do so without some alteration in our manner of functioning. The capacity to dream then, it would seem, is a crucial activity important for the functioning of the organism.

might also acknowledge the potentiality of a self that stands outside experience in the *day* dream and observes and evaluates and interprets—which plays with experience rather than in it. Life consists, suggests Christopher Bollas, of two complementary and perhaps interdependent selves that facilitate a person's processing of life according to different modes of engagement. What Bollas (1992, 27) refers to as the simple self ("when we are immersed in desired or evoked experience") is that position that endures the deep experiences in the dream or in life. It moves unself-consciously amongst objects that the ego has selected. It experiences the dream deeply, but it cannot know the dream. The complex self ("when we think about experience") has as its purpose to objectify as best as possible where the simple self has been or what is meant by the actions of the simple self in the dream. It can, unlike this simple self, know the dream but cannot experience it. The dream space is the space of play for the complex self; it is a "transitional space which a child (or adult) establishes to discover his self and external reality" (Khan 1974, 315). The dream space is the construction of the complex self where the object might be used because it is made available for use.

The dream must be available to knowledge as well as experience, but to whom is that knowledge available and how does it become available? How is the dream space created? Bollas (1992) argues that the complex self comes into being when the absolute immersion in the subjective experience is for some reason diminished. Perhaps as Dennett (1992) suggests, some impingement permits some withdrawal of cathexes so that the self immersed in experience can be seen by the complex self. It is this which occurs when we are driving and suddenly realize that we have not been paying attention to the road and yet remain unscathed. There are moments in our dream when we know we are dreaming. Then this complex self can behold the simple self as the protagonist of this dream moving about in a theater of its represented parts and can then reflect upon and interpret the dream.[2] The complex self provides the person

---

[2] I have discussed elsewhere (Block 1995) how Daniel Dennett's (1992) multiple drafts theory of consciousness might explain the creation of reality. Dennett's model begins with visual stimuli, but I believe the dream vision, which is not technically seen, might also be understood as a first stage.

another mode with which to process life than does the simple experiencing self, and it may do so according to a different yet interdependent mode of engagement: as the simple self experiences the dream, the complex self will permit the person to understand where she has been and what has been meant by her actions in the dream. The subject will come into existence. This event occurs in a space. "Each of our days begins to achieve its symbolic status as the dialectic between our unconscious wishes, needs, defenses, anxieties, and elaboratory self states engages with chance as the environment telephones us, writes to us, weathers us, offers us new books, displays wonderful-looking people, and so on. We might say, then, that the day space may be equivalent to the dream space" (Bollas 1992, 26). Both spaces, as I will suggest, must be understood as constructions established as an intermediate area for play. As we do during sleep in the dream, during the day we choose objects and are chosen—even allow ourselves to be chosen—by objects that elicit our particular psychic states. We realize those states by the choice of objects.

The construction of subjectivity depends on reflexivity. What is reflected upon is the nonunitary, multifaceted complex self: "I have hundreds, thousands, by my death millions of sequential self states arising from the dialectical meetings between my self and the object world . . ." (Bollas 1992, 29). What results from this process is "I." I read a specific book and not another; I read rather than write; I write academic prose rather than poetry; I imagine my academic prose is poetry. As in the dream, during the day we oscillate between the simple self and the complex self, the self wholly engaged in experience and the self that stands slightly back from the experience and reflects upon it—to discover where it has been and who it is. The dream—and reality—derive from what the mind does with objects since objects are all we have in the world with which to work. But they must be recognized as objects by the subject, and that is accomplished in the dream space.

Now, as I have said, the capacity to play demands space. Winnicott (1986, 36) has defined this space as the place of culture. It is a constructed area where the child or adult makes out of the objects of the world what s/he would. "Where do we find this third life of cultural experience? I think it cannot be placed in the inner or personal psychical reality, because it is not a dream—it is part of shared reality. But it cannot be said to be part of external relationships, because it is dominated by dream." Awareness of this simple self—the self immersed in experience—may be accomplished in the created space by the complex, reflective self that for some reason has withdrawn some energy from the subjective involvement in experience and can observe the simple self. The dream space is the construction of the complex self. "Recollection and interpretation of the dream's meaning do not necessarily address the essence of self experience gained by the simple self's movement through the events of the dream, but the complex self possesses a different psychic agenda: the aim of this position is to objectify as best as possible where one has been or what is meant by one's actions" (Bollas 1992, 15). These dreams offer the complex self visions of her own unconscious—of the true self. In dreams self can be experienced. Bollas (1992, 21) says that "The mnemic object is a particular form of subjective object that contains a projectively identified self experience, and when we use it, something of that self state stored in it will arise." The dream contains objects—even the represented self as object—and the choice of objects and the use of them are evocations of the self. "Dreams are an intelligence of form that holds, moves, stimulates, and shapes us" (1992, 14).

This space might also be conceptualized as what Marion Milner (1987, 70-82) refers to as the "framed gap." The frame is that construction that marks off what is inside from what is outside: the framed gap is the space in which play is possible as long as the materials are malleable. The framed gap is necessary if there is to be play at all; without a frame there can be no painting. The frame represents the constructed space in which creativity may develop. For Milner, the ability to paint derived from the confusion between what was inside (the dream) from what was outside (material world), derived from the inability to portray precisely what she saw or to represent wholly and exactly what was in one's mind. The inability to paint is a result of confusion of outlines or boundaries—what belongs to the world and what belongs to me. The framed gap is that marked off space that facilitates contemplative action in which "what we perceive has to be taken as symbol, as metaphor, not literally" (Milner 1987, 81). After all, the frame is an imposition separating what is inside from what is outside. That is, the construction of the dream space represents the Reality of embracing the reality between what one looks at and what one produces out of what one sees. In the construction of the dream space, the dreamer experiences the self who in the dream has experienced the dream. In the construction of the dream space the dreamer can distance him or herself from the dream itself and not be possessed by it. The frame represents the construction by the complex self; it is the acknowledgment and frame of the theater. The framed gap is the establishment of the dream space. It is the space for play. Play is the essence of creativity.

Playing is the use of the object and is the origin of creativity. Lev Vygotsky (1978) argues that play is central to the development of higher order psychological processes. Play permits the child to give meaning to what is not there. He states that "it is the essence of play that a new relation is created between the field of meaning and the visual field—that is between situations in thought and real situations" (1978, 104). Play is a liberating activity, freeing the self from the constraints of the immediate and the immediacy. "In the activity of play, things lose their determining force and are malleable. *The child sees one thing but acts differently in relation to what he sees, thus a condition is reached where the child begins to act independently of what he sees*" (Vygotsky 1978, 97). Dreaming might be considered a form of play; it is the evocation of the experiencing self out of the chaos of forms. From the myriad objects in the world certain ones are chosen, and the self is engaged in experience. From that experiencing self the reflective self may derive.

Dreaming is the creative use of objects to evoke self. Winnicott (1984, 95) notes that "The child who can manage dreams is becoming ready for all kinds of playing, either alone or with other children." As I have discussed elsewhere (Block 1995), it is impossible to produce a reality wholly from within, for our self-experiencing must always be placed in material objects that could never wholly replicate our subjectivity; nor can we produce a reality wholly from the recreation of the external. Our creations must always be a product of making something out of what we are given. Milner (1987, 84) notes that symbol formation of which we must consider the objects of the dream as representatives, are created "driven by the internal necessity for inner organization, pattern, coherence, the basic need to discover identity in differences without which experience becomes chaos." It is in the use of the object that playing occurs; it is in playing that creativity is realized. "Every object is a 'found' object. Given the chance, the baby begins to live creatively, and to use actual objects to be creative into and with" (Winnicott 1971, 101). The child must be able to use the dream creatively; it must be available for play.

Play is activity. Winnicott (1971, 41) says that "To control what is outside one has to *do* things, not simply to think or to wish, and *doing things takes time*. Playing is doing." It is not play to do with the object what it has been ordered to do; rather, playing is to do with the object what we will because it is available for use. "Playing," Winnicott (1971, 41) says, "is neither inside by any use of the word [which would be fantasy] . . . nor is it outside, that is, it is not a part of the repudiated world, the not-me, that which the individual has decided to recognize (with whatever difficulty and even pain) as truly external which is outside magical control." Playing, rather, is the interweave between the subjective and the objective, the negotiation between the true-self as potential and the objects it may use, ". . . between the inner reality of the individual and the shared reality of the world external to individuals" (Winnicott 1971, 64). Dreaming night and day produces self, as I have said, as the unconscious ego structures (the subjective) use objects (the objective) invested with energy to evoke a self. In dreams the self is represented not only by the subjective presence in the dream (the dreamer immersed in experience) but by the dream events and other aspects of the dream script (the objects in the dream). Hence the importance of manifest content—the actual matter of the dream. But the ability to use an object depends on the ability to play. In play the complex self finds what it creates because, in play, that self exists in an environment where its omnipotence—the capacity to find what it creates with impunity—is accepted. The ability to use the object—to construct the dream space—depends on the facilitating environment—on the caregivers. In order to use the object of the dream, my daughters must withdraw slightly from the total subjective involvement with it and construct this space wherein they might play. But they must be confident that in their use of the object it will yet survive their destruction of it; that is, that subsequent to its use the object will require no large-scale reparative work. The ability to use the dream depends upon the capacity to construct the dream space; this is the work of the complex self and is the mark of creativity. What is created is the reflective life that makes of objects what can be made out of them.

On the Facilitating Environment

Perhaps it is that the subjectivity of my infant daughter is yet in its infancy; she has in the dream the means to evoke the self in a moment. I, however, lack the capacity to know that subjectivity though I may interpret it. My interpretation will have lasting effect on her object relations (her psychic structures), her capacity for object use, and therefore, the development of her creativity. My interpretive capacities constitute the facilitating environment for my infant daughter; later, there will be, as there are for my six-year-old, other facilitating environments in which interpretive capacities are required and learned. School is one of these environments. If play is not possible in the dream space, if the facilitating environment precludes the possibility of play, then creativity is denied.

> A baby can be *fed* without love, but loveless or impersonal *management* cannot succeed in producing a new autonomous human child. Here where there is trust and reliability is a potential space, one that can become an infinite area of separation, which the baby, child, adolescent, adult may creatively fill with playing, which in time becomes the enjoyment of the cultural heritage (Winnicott 1971, 108).

It is then the function of the facilitating environment that permits the construction of the space.

If the dream must be used as an object, it must be available for that use. It is the construction of the dream space—the framed gap—that makes the dream an available object. The capacity to use the dream depends on the facilitating environment, an environment in which play is fostered. Masud Khan (1974, 311) writes, "I wish to suggest that the capacity to *use* the dream-mechanisms and the dream itself as a psychic experience is the result of adequate environmental provisions that facilitate the phase-adequate maturational processes." The dreamer must feel secure in the environment as s/he once did as the object of the caregivers' unconsciousness. "If a child feels that his subjectivity is held by some container, composed of the actual holding environment of parental care and subsequently the evolving structure of his own mind, then the subjectifying of the world feels licensed, underwritten and guaranteed" (Bollas 1992, 53). As I have said, the subjective self is immersed wholly in the dream. In a sense there is a quality of lostness about this immersion: the subjective self is, as it were, caught up in the whirlwind (see Michael Eigen 1992) out of which the complex self *in its reflexivity* may deliver it. The subjective self must feel a certain confidence that the environment in which it functions is secure enough to allow total engrossment in experience. For to be "immersed in the projective subjectification of reality [is] a chaos of forms, as we dissolve consciousness, disseminate parts of the self in units of experience, are evoked by objects that arrive by chance, and in turn use objects as lexical elements in the elaboration of idiom" (Bollas 1992, 53).

To engage in experience in this full manner requires total loss of self-objectivity. The ability to use the dream, as I have suggested, requires that this chaos be available to reflection. "Knowing that we will awaken from our dreaming, that we shall endure episodes of self observation and analysis, helps the individual to trust in the wisdom of surrender to subjectifications" (Bollas 1992, 53). Object relations theorists argue that this confidence is situated originally in the holding environment that permits a sense of what Winnicott terms "unintegration." It may be, as recent researchers have discovered, that this state of unintegration is not as Winnicott has described, but it is clear that the infant must feel secure in total subjectivity. Milner refers to this state as "reverie," the total loss of boundaries between the seer and the seen. To engage in this reverie in the creative dream demands (Milner 1987, 231)

the necessity of a certain quality of protectiveness in the environment. For there are obviously many circumstances in which it is not safe to be absent-minded; it needs a setting, both physical and mental. It requires a physical setting in which we are freed, for the time being, from the need for immediate practical expedient action; and it requires a mental setting, an attitude, both in the people around and in oneself, a tolerance of something which may at moments look very like madness.

The dreamer, the experiencing self, must first be confident that it may come out of the state and reflect on it in safety. The holding environment must be such that the experiencing self's use of it will not result in retaliation for its actions in it. The infant must learn that though it destroys the object, which includes the environment, the object remains. If, on the other hand, the individual does not feel this confidence, or if the environment is indeed, destructible, then the individual is also not secure to release its elements to self-experiencing; the intra-psychic processes are disrupted and the dream will not be available for reflection. Rather, the self is too threatened for such abandonment.

In this regard it may be interesting to consider Joel Kovel's (1987, 336) idea of schizophrenia not as a disorder that occurs to being but rather as a form of object relation to and object use of the self not unlike that which produces and takes place in the dream.[3] Schizophrenia, for Kovel, is the active work of the self trying to maintain its integrity in the face of a frightening loss of identity and a diminishing sense of the locus of subjectivity. The aetiology of schizophrenia seems situated in a disruption of object relations and the incapacity to reconstruct those relations. The self disintegrates. Objects may be used but in ways that are uneconomical. Schizophrenia, Kovel argues, is not something that merely happens to the ego. Rather, schizophrenia is an annihilation of being; it represents the attempt to reconstruct that being, often with catastrophic results. Thus, the schizophrenic cannot withdraw cathexis from the subjective participation in the dream because there is no self to observe the self in the dream. There is no stance from which to view the experiencing self. The schizophrenic enacts his/her sense that "I am ceasing to exist, the me-ness that circum-

---

[3] Indeed, what we learn from the work of Oliver Sacks (1985; 1995) is that in its breakdown we learn about the structures of the human mind and personality.

scribes the elemental sense of what it is to live a life is going, if not already gone, something unspeakably violent is transpiring . . . and as I cease to exist for myself, a bounded creature moving with a world of other creatures, I find parts of my scattered self in the world, while parts of the world come to occupy spaces of nonbeing within the self" (Kovel 1987, 336).

Now this feeling of what Winnicott refers to as unintegration, and that might be understood as willed chaos, is the matrix out of which creation might come. But the schizophrenic, unlike the artist, is incapable of remaking the world that has been destroyed; rather, the schizophrenic is obsessed with "desperate restitution of the shattered subject." This shattering is inexplicable (Kovel says: "Something happens[4] that cannot be named and that ruptures the experienced place of a person in the universe"), and it entails the loss of object relations—the inability to make something anew—and the desperate but futile attempt to make reconnections. The schizophrenic's nightly dream occurs, but there is no complex self to observe and interpret. Rather, the schizophrenic seeks objects to use but cannot first establish relations that are explicable or communicable. There is no one or thing to relate to in the world. In Khan's terms, the schizophrenic cannot construct the dream space.

To my mind the schizophrenic condition is further evidence that object relating is central to being. In the case of the schizophrenic, Kovel (1987, 341) argues, his/her relations to others are "outside the social contract . . . marked by very poor economic and political adaptation." Hence, though contact with the environment seems crucial for the restitution of being in the schizophrenic, in fact there is no one in the technocratic society to reach out to the schizophrenic. We will return to this point later in our discussion of the school. But for now we must note that in schizophrenia the waking dream lacks subjectivity; the schizophrenic cannot talk to another subject because she is not present to do so.

Now perhaps, it is argued, in the latter part of the twentieth century we are all are schizoid personalities. And so it is possible that in our waking dream we all partake of the

---

[4] I am reminded of Joseph Heller's novel *Something Happens*.

symptomology of the schizophrenic. Certainly in the dream
we permit our selves to experience the chaos of forms. Masud
Khan (1974) notes that the history of psychoanalysis is, in part,
the "changing clinical picture of our patients." Whereas earlier, say for Freud and the early psychoanalysts, the model patient was considered hysteric or obsessionally neurotic, Khan
notes that the patient presenting himself in analysis more recently is the schizoid personality. Kovel situates this schizophrenic condition in the environment of the technocratic society that cannot support the nonproductive nature of the
schizophrenic. "For all its wealth and power, capitalist society
turns out to be one of the worst settings possible in which to
be schizophrenic . . . it conspires to predispose, precipitate,
and maintain the condition in its most malignant form" (Kovel
1987, 341). Akin to Kovel's thesis, Khan notes that the schizoid
personality is one in which the developing self was not given
sufficient support and therefore had to develop a false self to
protect the true self. This false self becomes the nurturer of
the true self, but it can never become a true self itself. Quot-
ing Fairbairn, Khan notes that we all are inevitably schizoid in
that everyone must experience splits in the ego and manifest
the false self. Kovel states that the more drastic forms of schizophrenia (see Willa Cather's story, "Paul's Case") are an actual
shattering of the self. Khan speaks about the borderline schizophrenic, Kovel of the more severe. In both Kovel's and Khan's
theorizing, however, a sense of object relations is disturbed; it
may be at least one function of the dream to mirror or to address this disturbance. Perhaps if the schizophrenic could speak
the dream, the condition might find relief. Bollas (1992, 14)
says that

> the productive intentionality that determines the dream we are in and
> that never reveals itself (i.e., "where is the dreamer that dreams the
> dream?") uncannily re-creates . . . the infant's relation to the mother's
> unconscious, which although it does not "show itself," nonetheless
> produces the process of maternal care. In this respect the dream seems
> to be a structural memory of the infant's unconscious, an object rela-
> tion of person inside the other's unconscious processing, revived in
> the continuous representation of the infantile moment every night.

In the dream we may deconstruct ourselves in the safety of the
mother's unconsciousness. In the dream we are "loosed into

an archipelago of many beings, acting various roles scripted by the ego in the theater of the night." When we awaken we can reflect on the different selves we have had experience of in the dream. The schizophrenic, perhaps, is not capable of a letting loose of the self in dream because its facilitating environment is not there. Nor can the schizophrenic reflect on the dream when out of it because there is no subjectivity to do so. Thus, it is possible that the schizophrenic's dreams may be healthful but can serve no function.

It is in the dream space where creativity may be explored and realistically created. The ability to use the object depends on the belief in the object's indestructibility. Objects may only be used—may only be creatively used—if they are capable of withstanding destruction; they must survive our aggressiveness. Adam Phillips (1993, 39) asserts that creativity "involved the search for, and attempt to establish, a medium, an environment, a relationship that could survive the person's most passionate destructiveness." If the object survives our destructiveness, then the object is real and may be loved. The early aggressiveness referred to above, which is merely energy, becomes linked to destructiveness from which guilt may arise. The guilt that derives from these early aggressive drives turns with the object's survival to concern and love: as Winnicott (1965, 82) says, "the anxiety about the id drives and the fantasy of these drives becomes tolerable to the baby, who can then experience guilt, or can hold it in full expectation of an opportunity to make reparation for it. To this guilt that is held but not felt as such, we give the name 'concern.'" Hence in play we can experience concern for the object. Concern—morality—grows out of play and is not a prerequisite for it. It is the facilitating environment that makes possible this testing and the growth of care. It is the environment that permits the construction of the dream space. What I am talking about is the classroom and the curriculum.

Education as the Stuff of Dreams

I read in the newspapers that American education requires more rigorous and carefully defined standards if it is to produce students who will enable continued competition in the

world marketplace of the twenty-first century. I understand
that a large percentage of the jobs that our children will enter
have not yet been invented. I am told that although crime in
the streets has decreased, crime in the schools is on the rise.
Reports announce that drop-out rates increase as tuitions rise
and scholarship opportunities diminish. Affirmative action
programs are eliminated. Suicide, it is announced, is the leading cause of death of children. Our schools, we are told, must
demand more of our students. I don't know what that means. I
walk in the halls of the school buildings and I peek in the win-
dows and listen at the doors. On the chalkboards are lessons,
homework assignments, and teacher writings. At their desks
students sit immobile and barely conscious. Or worse: confined,
they sit immersed in the waking nightmare of fears instilled by
the desire to explore and the strictures of the school that deny
play, risk-taking, and creativity. No holding environment this;
rather, school is conceptualized, structured, and operated as a
holding tank prior to release into the equally constrained world.
I sit in a fourth grade class and marvel that I can discover no
reason for the children to talk in here. At a school play the
script is read by a professional actor on cassette tape. The children sit motionless behind scenery. The silence is frightening.

I am reminded of Timon's exasperation in Disney's *The Lion
King*. For Timon, the clever meerkat, recent events suggest a
world wholly irrational, dangerously contingent and absurd,
and yet no one seems the least bit concerned. The easeful life
of Hakuna Matata has been dramatically and terrifyingly ended
by the intrusion of real danger from without. Despite the new
vision of a threatening world, no one but Timon expresses concern. Pumbaa, the warthog, has just been saved by Simba from
being eaten by the lioness, Nala, and suddenly the two lions,
Simba and Nala, are cuddling and nuzzling like lovers. The easy
life that Timon, Pumbaa, and Simba had lived as a private (albeit male) trio is ended with Nala's endangering entrance into
their community. Yet to Timon's impassioned dismay no one
seems alarmed. "Hey," Timon screams, "what's going on here.
Hey, what's going on here? Time out!! Let me get this straight!!
You know her. She knows you. But she wants to eat him and
everybody's okay with this. Did I miss something?" These are
my questions too: What is going on here? Did I miss some-

thing? If what is occurring in schools is okay but we just need more of it, then how can I explain to myself much less to my daughters the horrifying realities I daily observe of school life? If rigorous standards in a discrete curriculum are set to ensure the continued prominence of American productivity and business hegemony, then how do I explain the growing number of homeless and the increasingly desperate state of hungry children and lonely older citizens? If a fervent nationalism is driving our educational priorities (see Patrick Buchanan, William Buckley, Bill Clinton, or Bob Dole for variations on this theme), then how will I explain to our children Somalia, Bosnia-Herzegovina, or the Middle East? When I read to my daughter *The Diary of Anne Frank*, what do I answer when she asks if they will come for her? Is there anything about school or education that should make her feel safe? "Hey, what's going on here? Did I miss something?"

I recall from my adolescence a song recorded by the Chad Mitchell Trio. It is a satire. Barely. It is titled "The Merry Minuet" and was written by Sheldon Harnick:

> They're rioting in Africa
> They're starving in Spain
> There's hurricanes in Florida
> And Texas needs rain
>
> The whole world is festering with unhappy souls
> The French hate the Germans the Germans hate the Poles
> Italians hate Yugoslavs, South Africans hate the Dutch
> And I don't like anybody very much.

What was true in 1958 when this song was written is still true in 1995. It may be that this is the world in which I have lived for my fifty years, but it seems absurd to believe that this is the world I must perpetuate for my children. If education is organized to assert and maintain America's primacy in the world market, then I despair for our children. I despair for our teachers. "Life for us," Alfie Kohn (1992, 1) writes, "has become an endless succession of contents. From the moment the alarm clock rings until sleep overtakes us again, from the time we are toddlers until the day we die, we are busy struggling to outdo others. This is our posture at work and at school, on the playing field and back at home. It is the common denominator of

American life." If it is the intent of Goals 2000, a Clinton proposal, to perpetuate and enhance this grasping, then I whole-
heartedly oppose the plan. However, I approve of at least one
of the tenets of Goals 2000. That document declares that by
the year 2000 every child will attend school ready to learn. I
take that to mean that every mother will have prenatal care
available as a right, that every father and mother will have worth-
while employment that will help fulfill their own lives so they
might provide a facilitating environment for the growth of their
children. In this way every child will live and learn with stom-
achs filled with foods that enable growth. Goals 2000 means to
me that high quality day-care will be available to every family
regardless of income level. Goals 2000 promises universal and
comprehensive health care. Whom am I kidding? The real
agenda of Goals 2000, I know, is the increasing politicization
of childhood, the imposition of more rigorous standards for
younger and younger children, and the cloaking of our politi-
cians in sheep's clothing all for the benefit of the market
economy. What are we to do? What is to be done?

It is time to drastically rethink the very purposes for which
education is organized and, thus, to reconceptualize the children who are its objects. They must be permitted to become
again subjects that they might become their own objects. I believe with David Purpel (1995) that

> As educators we should not be merely committed to education, we
> should instead be more deeply committed to human dignity; we should
> not dedicate ourselves to higher learning but to a high standard of
> living for all; our responsibilities are not to select the best students
> but to eradicate privilege; our commitment must not be to the market
> economy but to the Golden Rule. It is idolatrous to commit oneself
> primarily to the preservation of History, Biology, or any other disci-
> pline or field where there is injustice, inequality, and hatred in the
> land. We need not be concerned with a decline in test scores; we need
> to be outraged and obsessed with an increase in unnecessary human
> suffering. As educators we must not offer justice, joy, and love
> as rewards or luxuries but affirm them as requirements for a life of
> meaning.

I believe that it is possible to rethink the nature of schooling
to promote the type of spiritual and moral values so eloquently
voiced above without sacrificing the highly rigorous and com-

plete education so adamantly demanded by all. And I believe that Dewey was correct to suggest that the curriculum needs to be returned to the child, which is to say that it is from the authority of the child that curriculum must develop. As Howard Gardner suggests (1991), the unschooled mind develops knowledge in the absence of schooling, and the best schooling cannot replace this foundation without extensive archaeological study of these structures. In this chapter I have suggested that our beings are based in object relations and that we may evoke being and be evoked by object use. We must begin to focus not on the materials that pass as knowledge but on what is done with that material. Christopher Bollas (1989, 94) writes that the psychoanalyst's ideas become the "provision of objects that can be used by the patient to evoke repressed memories, to collect split thoughts, or to facilitate new self states. It is *the patient's use of* such objects that determines whether an idea becomes an insight." I am not suggesting that teachers be psychoanalysts, though some rigorous training for all in that discipline might serve education better than many of the courses now required in teacher education programs. But what I suggest is that all the teacher's knowledge is only potential knowledge: it is only an object that must be used by the student to generate knowledge in him/herself. What use any object may entail depends on the personal idiom and the facilitating or nonfacilitating environment that the school and classroom prepare. My daughter may read the story of Cinderella as a metaphor for the decline of western civilization, but it is only my function to discover how she makes what she will of that story. I can correct her if I have the will, but then I have denied her play and creativity, given her an object with which she may not play, and I have myself become an object set in opposition and thereby threatening to her. When I tell her that the shirt on her head is only a shirt and not long flowing hair, I do more than end her game; I deny her.

Madeleine Grumet (1988, 172) writes that "In order for curriculum to provide the moral, epistemological, and social situations that allow persons to come to form, it must provide the ground for their action rather than their acquiescence." I have tried to show what that coming to form might mean, and I have tried to suggest how the ground might be conceptualized.

On the one hand the simple self must be immersed in experience so that it might realize its idiom. It must have objects available that it might use; it must feel secure enough within the environment that it might play. Play must be facilitated in the classroom in activities that will be educative. Marion Milner (1987, 101) writes that "It is the capacity of the environment to foster this growth, by providing conditions in which a recurrent partial return to the feeling of being one is possible; and I suggest that the environment does this by the recurrent providing of a framed space and time and a pliable medium, so that, on occasions, it will not be necessary for self-preservation's sake to distinguish between inner and outer, self and not-self." The classroom might be conceptualized as this framed space or gap on which the student's work might be created. If it is not so conceived, then education is a paint-by-numbers experience. We color in by demand what others have already drawn. There is no play there, only tedious and meaningless rote work.

I believe that the willingness of the students to immerse themselves in experience depends on the confidence that there will be time and space to withdraw from the experience and reflect upon it. The inability to withdraw slightly might lead to feeling possessed by the structure and be, therefore, incapable of using it. What I have referred to as the complex self—the Deweyan reflective self—must have the freedom and capacities to observe that self within experience. In the parlance of this chapter, the simple self must be available to the complex self as an object. Thus it is that the school must serve as a holding environment permitting students to create their world in activity and as the activity of education. In such an environment students would have the freedom to explore in a safe atmosphere that supports their exploration. When the environment is established for their safety—and by this I mean not only their physical safety, as out on the playground or the chemistry laboratory, but also their emotional well-being and development—then children will act on the seemingly innate drive to be part of community. The classroom must provide that assurance as well. And I believe that the traditional canon of knowledge might even be part of that security. It is at least available as potential moments of insight.

So this is not to argue that the classroom and the school ought to be thoroughly undisciplined venues. This unwarranted view of progressive education is predicated on the present structures of schools: it assumes the priority of the traditional classroom with the teacher as leader. It assumes a canon of knowledge that must be acquired. It assumes a necessity for hierarchical ordering that demands the awarding of grades. It homogenizes. It harms children by deforming them. The Jewish philosopher Emmanuel Levinas (1994, 16) writes that "One may speak of oppression even in a perfectly just state, precisely because the relation of the I to the universality that recognizes but defines it passes inevitably through an administration." And we cannot even believe that we live in a perfectly just state.

Rather, we must rethink the spaces in which we educate our young. Howard Gardner writes eloquently on this when he speaks of the museum as the early site of education for our children. In this conceptualization, he addresses the concerns I have raised in this chapter by providing for a vast array of objects and a freedom for their use in an unstructured and noncompetitive environment but one in which the objects of this world are offered for play (Gardner 1991, 202):

> Imagine an educational environment in which youngsters at the age of seven or eight, in addition to—or perhaps instead of—attending a formal school, have the opportunity to enroll in a children's museum, a science museum, or some kind of discovery center or exploratorium. As part of this educational scene, adults are present who actually practice the disciplines or crafts represented by the various exhibitions. Computer programmers are working in the technology center, zookeepers and zoologists are tending the animals, workers from a bicycle factory assemble bicycles in front of the children's eyes, and a Japanese mother prepares a meal and carries out a tea ceremony in the Japanese house. Even the designers and mounters of the exhibitions ply their trade directly in front of the observing students.

Each object—and ideas are indeed objects—that can be used may facilitate new self states. It is in the use of objects that education may occur. At present there are very few uses of the objects of the school. It is no wonder that our schools are a failure. We must reconsider the notions of school and schooling. If our being is founded in object relations and realized in object use, then we must foster activity and action in the school.

As I have conceptualized it, we can only elaborate our idiom in an object world. "Each individual is unique, and the true self is an idiom of organization that seeks its personal world through the use of an object. As the person views a potential object field, he sights objects that are of interest to him, and this procedure necessitates his thoughtless discarding of certain objects in favour of objects of desire. This is true whether the person is searching for a partner, browsing in a bookshop, or listening to a symphony" (Bollas 1989, 110). It is true as well if the person him/herself is the object sought. I think the aesthetic basis of life consists of articulating one's idiom and achieving subjectivity.

By subject I refer to Bollas' use of the term: "the subject is what comes into being when one finds the means to express one's inner status in the moment, unhindered by the knowledge that no such subjective state shall ever escape the problematics of unconscious context" (1989, 53). Coming to subjectivity depends on the ability to use the dream. It occurs in reflection. Now, Freud offered ways in which we might read our unconscious; Richard Rorty (1989, 32) says that Freud's vocabulary "permits us to sketch narrative of our own development, our idiosyncratic moral struggle, which is more finely textured, far more custom-tailored to our individual case, than the moral vocabulary which the philosophical tradition offered regarding one's purpose and one's place in the world." We might, Rorty suggests, use Freud's vocabulary to elaborate our individual chronicle. It is that narrative, Bollas (1987, 9) tells us, that accounts for the idea of self: "The person's self is the history of many internal relations. Each infant, child, adolescent and adult (through the life cycle) experiences the—theoretically infinite—parts of the self articulated through the interplay of internal and external reality. Once any one part is objectified (in thought or feeling) it thereupon comes into existence." The struggle Rorty refers to and the narrative referred to by Bollas, as object-relations theory tells us, derive from the relationship we establish with the world about us, through the evocation of selves through the use of objects. Already, feminist and postformal educators offer curriculum that not only advocates this ontological position steeped in issues of race, gender, and class but offers environments for its study as well.

The work of William Pinar (1994) is a model for this form of education. So too is the work of Joe Kincheloe "Critical constructivists," Kincheloe (1993, 36) writes, "perceive a socially constructed world and ask what are the forces that shape our constructions. Our constructions of reality are freely made but are shaped by power interests in the larger society."[5] Constructivists acknowledge that the world is our construction; critical constructivists seek the self's enmeshment in the world, seek the self in the world and the world in the self. As Prospero admits to Ferdinand, constructivists attribute psychological states to the individual's relations to objects and not to the objects themselves: "Sir," he assures Ferdinand to explain his apparent aggravation, "I am vex'd./Bear with my weakness" (IV,i,158-59). This acknowledgment, constructivists argue, permits the self to emerge. "Emotional and psychological realities bring with them self states which become part of our history. The concept of self should refer to the positions or point of view from which and through which we sense, feel, observe and reflect on distinct separate experiences in our being" (Bollas 1987, 10). The self is several selves that comprise the subject, and the expression of any one self depends on the objects available. There is no doubt of the political nature of self nor of the politics of object relations theory. Rather, it is acknowledged from the start and implicit in acknowledgment of self construction. Later Prospero will from his strength remake the world and reestablish his reign as Prince.[6] Prospero's position is very much akin to constructivism: knowledge derives from our construction of it and is not a reading of it in

---

[5] Karl Marx (1963, 15) as I suggested in the previous chapter, had earlier expressed a similar point of view: "Men make their own history but they do not make it just as they please; they do not make it under circumstances chosen by themselves, but under circumstances directly encountered, given and transmitted from the past. The tradition of all the dead generations weighs like a nightmare on the brain of the living."

[6] To his traitorous brother Prospero says:
> For you, most wicked sir, whom to call brother
> Would even infect my mouth, I do forgive
> Thy rankest fault—all of them; and require
> My dukedom of thee, which perforce I know
> Thou must restore.

the world. Wisdom is knowing that we understand little but that knowledge is forever possible. "Decentered by experience, radically historicized, not given integrating memories neatly unifying the nature of life, we are nonetheless inhabited by the *revenants* of the dream work of life, thousands of inner constellations of psychic realities, each conjurable by name or memory, even if few are truly intelligible" (Bollas 1992, 61). We are such stuff as dreams are made on. We might teach our students to deconstruct the dream, but we must first permit them the free construction of it that it might be used.

Rorty (1989, 68) argues from a parallel position in pragmatic philosophy that the traditional notion of epistemology about which our schools are today governed ought to be replaced with the notion of politics so that the conditions that would clarify the idea of truth as correspondence to reality might gradually be replaced by the idea of truth as what comes to be believed in the course of free and open encounters. In this conversation, the construction of reality—to make of the world what we would—would obtain from our ability to engage in free and open discourse to make of the world what we would. It would obtain, I argue, from play, from the use of objects in an environment that is facilitating. The world is substantial, alright, it is just not Reality. We would know whence our world derives and how we daily add psychic structures that make us more complex, thereby increasing our capacity to establish the dream work of life the construction of which further extends our notion of reality that is ultimately available to us for use. Schools ought to facilitate this construction.

"In dreams," Thoreau (1961, 371) writes, "we see ourselves naked and acting out our real characters, even more clearly than we see others awake." I have tried to explore the dream as the expression of self and to suggest how this self immersed in experience may be observed. The self in the dream is lost in moments of intense activity in which awareness of self and awareness of the object are fused. To emerge from the dream is to discover that a new entity has been created. I have suggested that the exemplar of the dream might apply to waking life and that this oscillation between immersion and separation might result in the construction of knowledge. And I have suggested that the possibilities of movement and the ability to engage in experience depend on the holding environment of which the school must be known as a crucial site.

We are such stuff as dreams are made on. Dream a little dream of me. Life is but a dream. It's alright, ma, I'm only bleeding.

Chapter V

Walking and Curriculum

On Walking: Some Thoughts on Hansel and Gretel

Henry David Thoreau (1980, 94) declares, "If you are ready to leave father and mother, and brother and sister, and wife and child and friends, and never see them again—if you have paid your debts, and made your will, and settled all your affairs, and are a free man, then you are ready for a walk." Now it is clear to me that for Thoreau a walk was not an innocent or superficial occasion, though I suspect that for him it might be characterized by a quality of leisure.[1] Rather, Thoreau's walk was the engagement in a momentous, energetic event from which return was certainly not a consummation devoutly to be wished. For Henry David Thoreau, to take a walk was to redefine the relationships that constituted the identity of the walker. To take a walk was to be engaged in educative experience. May Sarton (1973) also understood the seriousness of the walk; she held that to take a walk was to resume old conversations and to reconnect the self to others. Sarton's walk recognizes the necessity of walking for growth and learning and is undertaken when the self no longer feels in touch with itself, with others, or with the world. The walk for Sarton was a conversation. In that reconnection she becomes herself remade. After such a Thoravian or Sartonian walk, the familiar becomes unfamiliar, the familial exotic, and the notion of home forever trans-

---

[1] Thoreau says, "The really efficient laborer will be found not to crowd his day with work, but will saunter to his task surrounded by a wide halo of ease and leisure."

formed. In that process the walker produces herself and her world. Such a walk appears to me to be the ideal model of education. On such a walk I would send my children.

In this regard I think of the Brothers Grimm who tell us that when Hansel and Gretel set out in the woods on that frightening and foreboding first night, Hansel took the precaution to drop shiny white pebbles along their path to mark the way home, as his father had carefully taught him to do. And when Hansel and Gretel were abandoned as they had expected to be by their father, the children were able—to their father's apparent surprise and delight—to follow the pebble-marked path and arrive back in their home by morning. I meditate often upon those pebbles dropped by the two children; upon walking; upon finding one's way back home; and upon education. It would seem that the walk in which we engage has influence on the learning in which we engage; the walking we do influences the walks on which we venture. Whom we may become is dependent on the walks we may undertake.

I would like to consider in this chapter what it might mean to take a walk, for it appears to me that walking might be considered at least a significant form of education if not considered to be the process of education itself.[2] It is true that at present and for the most part our children remain fairly sedentary for the greater portion of their schooling, and I am concerned about what effects might be secured in that inactivity. I am concerned about what education is achieved in that immobility, in a restraint of walking. And I would also like to consider the myriad ways that we have curricularly devised to keep children's walking constrained, stepping on prescribed paths, dropping little white pebbles, keeping themselves always mired in view, observed by the ceaseless trails of writing we have mandated and that define their position. I have discussed in the previous chapter how being occurs in an interaction with objects in an environment that is facilitating. I have suggested there that we express ourselves in our choice of objects; we evoke our selves in our choice of objects. If we severely restrict

---

[2] I am reminded of the walkabout that appears to be more a test of knowledge than an actual production of it, although in Nicholas Roeg's film *Walkabout*, the two white children do engage in active learning.

or, worse, deny altogether the availability of objects, what violence must we inevitably inflict upon the self? What education may be achieved in the organized procession of contemporary education where every object is externally chosen, its meaning always-already defined, and its use previously determined? It is, I think, a curious form of education that we practice, one that too often denies the very activity upon which education must be based.[3] We deny, indeed, the very possibility of education. To deny walking in its Thoravian or Sartonian sense, we mandate an education that precludes adventure, exploration, and self discovery and demands a conformity that deforms the evolving selves who are our children. It's alright, ma, I'm only bleeding.

I am cognizant of many such mechanisms in educational practice by which children are produced and controlled, indeed, produced by that control. We set paths for our children and impel them upon those paths; we deny the potential for self-impelled movement by determining every step along the prescribed ways and therefore deny the pleasures of discovery. We define the path, the pace, and the products and deny the exploration by which character is produced. Woe to them that deviate from those paths; woe to those that remain on them. In this process we call education, we deform the child's development and practice a form of social violence that underlies the very society in which we live. In this chapter I would like to explore this aspect of schooling and curriculum. Because it is, I believe, the curriculum of the schools—a prescribed body of knowledge and methods by which that knowledge might be communicated—that represents the uninterrupted path of writing that connects the center to the periphery, that serves as the pebbles by which the path is forged and marked that children might always find their way home even though the father

---

[3] John Dewey ([1902]1956, 31) writes, "Some years ago I was looking about the school supply stores in the city, trying to find desks and chairs which seemed thoroughly suitable from all points of view—artistic, hygienic and educational—to the needs of the children. We had a great deal of difficulty in finding what we needed, and finally one dealer, more intelligent than the rest, made this remark: I am afraid we have not what you want. You want something at which the children may work; these are all for listening."

has long since absented himself from that path, ensconced himself at home, and abandoned education for the thrill of exercising control by allowing the child to assume responsibility for it. It is no wonder that the father is delighted to see his children, Hansel and Gretel, again. No children, no control. Indeed, wasn't it he who taught them about the pebbles in the first place? I would like to suggest here that education occurs in activity—in the walking—and that without activity we deny education. Indeed, it is only when Hansel and Gretel get lost as they walk through the thick and strange woods that they are able to achieve any learning. Ultimately, in the walking becomes the walker. To deny the walking denies the walker as well. But, it's alright, ma, I'm only bleeding.

And so I would like to return to the notion of the walk, to the idea of home from which walks commence, and to the delineations of the paths on which we walk. I think we always walk from home; to what we return remains in question. Indeed, who returns is, as well, an issue. These are matters of process. I think that if education is to be effective, the exercise of the walk must produce a walker; that walker cannot be coincident with the fixed individual prior to the walk or to the stationary individual who refused to walk. If who returns is immediately recognizable on return, then what has occurred on the walk needs to be considered. If everything appears the same to the walker upon return from the walk then s/he must evaluate what change has actually occurred in the walker in the walking that could facilitate the establishment of new relationships. As it is now organized, education is a solitary and sedentary exercise and denies our children the rights of their own development. Our educational system denies much that we have learned from physiology and psychology and constrains our children's growth in a form of violence not the less insidious because it is so easily acquiesced to. It's alright, ma, I'm only bleeding.

If I Knew the Way, I Would Take You Home

Thoreau (1962, 83), a thoroughly disorienting teacher, knew a great deal about home and paths and walking and education. Indeed, as it has been suggested in the hagiography, Thoreau quit teaching rather than subject a child to requisite corporal punishment. For Thoreau education as it was then practiced—and is still—had nothing to do with freedom and learning. "What does education do?" he asks. "It makes a straight cut ditch of a free meandering brook." That free, meandering brook wanders through the world seeking objects by which it might evoke self. The straight cut ditch may not saunter, and its vistas remain severely restricted. Worse, the violence by which it must perforce be formed denies freedom by obliging direction and altering the nature and function of the brook. Education, Thoreau knew, should have nothing to do with marked paths and returning home. For Thoreau education has more to do with sauntering, with getting lost. He announces that it is but a "Two or three hours' walking will carry me to as strange a country as I expect ever to see" (Thoreau 1980, 101). Indeed, it is only when he is lost, he acknowledges, that he can find himself again. It is so easy to be lost in the world (save for in schools), he announces: one has only to turn about once in the world with the eyes closed to lose one's sense of place so as to be enabled to find it again. And once found, the walker is changed. Thoreau notes playfully (1961, 93) that the word saunterer derives from *sans terre*, "without land or a home, which, therefore, in the good sense, will mean, having no particular home, but equally at home everywhere." This is not the condition of education today nor its espoused ends. Indeed, the function of education, in the still relevant words of Horace Mann (1969, 50), is to "take the accumulations in knowledge, of almost six thousand years, and to transfer the vast treasure to posterity." More recently Paolo Freire ([1970]1985) referred to this practice as the banking concept of education; there are other insidious ways to perceive it.

In *Discipline and Punish* Michel Foucault (1979, 96) notes how the governors of plague-ridden Paris are able to maintain control over the city in order to deal with the pestilence by a system of surveillance "based on a system of permanent registration." They mean to control the plague by controlling the population. By a system of complete self-report, the administrators of the city can know the status of each of its citizens. This panopticonal mechanism, of which Bentham's model of the prison is the architectural representation, arranges everything so that the "surveillance is permanent in its effects, even if it is discontinuous in its action." The panopticonal apparatus is "a machine for creating and sustaining a power relation independent of the person who exercises it the effect of which is that the inmates are caught up in a power situation of which they themselves are the bearers" (Foucault 1979, 201). Aware that they can be always seen though unsure of when they are actually in view, the inmates begin to regulate their own behaviors. So too in plague-ridden Paris: confined to their homes for their own personal and social good, the populace is readily observable and perfectly controlled, controlled because they oversee themselves as the condition of being (Foucault 1979, 197):

> This enclosed, segmented space observed at every point, in which the individuals are inserted in a fixed place, in which the slightest movements are supervised, in which all events are recorded, in which an uninterrupted work of writing links the centre and periphery, in which power is exercised without division, according to a continuous hierarchical figure, in which each individual is constantly located, examined and distributed among the living beings, the sick and the dead—all this constitutes a compact model of the disciplinary mechanism. The plague is met by order.

What is created, of course, is a perfectly managing and controlling hierarchy participated in willingly by the subjected as the very means of their existence, as a process establishing individuality. Terry Eagleton (1990, 19) says, ironically I take it, that in such a system, "The liberated subject is the one who has appropriated the law as the very principle of its own autonomy, broken the forbidding tables of stone on which that law was originally inscribed in order to rewrite it on the heart of flesh. To consent to the law is thus to consent to one's own inward being." This panopticonal mechanism organized by a system of endless writing "lays down for each individual his place, his body, his disease and his death, his well-being by means of an omnipresent and omniscient power that subdivides itself in a regular, uninterrupted way even to the ultimate determination of the individual, or what characterizes him of what belongs to him . . . the panoptic mechanism arranges spatial unities that make it possible to see constantly and recognize instantly" (Foucault 1979, 202-3). This panopticon "reverses the principle of the dungeon; or rather, of its three functions—to enclose, to deprive of light, and to hide—it preserves only the first and eliminates the other two. Full lighting and the eye of a supervisor capture better than darkness, which ultimately protects. Visibility is a trap" (Foucault 1979, 200). I understand education as a form of panopticonal mechanism in which one is constantly in view and denied any hope of getting lost. Indeed, Michael Katz (1987) and David Nasaw (1979) have studied the development of the school and its bureaucracy as means of maintaining social control of education. In this mechanism, education is denied if, at a minimum, we mean by education the development of a self-aware consciousness, the conscious production of selfhood undertaken in relative freedom.

The school and its curriculum is such a panopticonal structure: it promotes incarceration by organizing visibility. In the school, children are defined by what they know; this knowledge is always linked to written reports that delimit and circumscribe that knowledge. Increasingly, what children know is often written by and for others. Children are always to be found by their position on the well-traveled, well-lit, and heavily marked path that is called the curriculum. Indeed, alternative paths are frowned upon if not altogether denied. Students measure themselves by their place on the prescribed educational paths. They are known by their IQ scores, their grade and grades, their SAT scores, and their grade point average. We test every aspect of a child that we might control its development. Foucault (1979, 202-3) writes that "He who is subjected to a field of visibility, and who knows it, assumes responsibility for the constraints of power; he makes them play spontaneously upon himself; he inscribes in himself the power relation which he simultaneously plays both roles; he becomes the principle of his own subjection." The endless stream of writing organizes the visibility of the populace and maintains control. My daughter's friend tells her that at her school, bathroom visits are permitted twice a day and at prescribed times. When my six-year-old-daughter says that the practice sounds unfair, her friend answers, "In fourth grade it is fair. I learn to hold it in." The mother of a *five-year-old* child cries in my office because it has been recommended that her daughter enroll in summer school because the child has been labeled insufficiently skilled in the recitation of the alphabet for entrance to kindergarten! A young father tells me that his *six-year-old son* has been prescribed ritalin for hyperactivity! It's alright, ma, I'm only bleeding.

Now I believe that education ought not to be a discipline, a movement progressively along a path cut and defined by others and by which our position along that path defines ourselves. Foucault (1979, 138) tells us:

> Discipline produces subjected and practised bodies, "docile" bodies. Discipline increases the forces of the body (in economic terms of utility) and diminishes these same forces (in political terms of obedience). In short, it dissociates power from the body; on the one hand, it turns it into an "aptitude," a "capacity," which it seeks to increase; on the other hand, it reverses the course of the energy, the power that might result from it, and turns it into a relation of strict subjection.

This is the movement of education today. It is defined in terms of standards and restrictions. Diane Ravitch (1995, 377) says that "standards will only have this effect [of educational reform] when a school, community, or state embraces high standards but also takes the necessary steps to realign curriculum, textbooks, assessments, and teacher training and education to them—so that the whole school or education system is consciously directing its energies toward the same goal." That goal, of course, is the achievement of externally imposed standards concerning what every student should know. Ravitch's prescription for education ensures the visibility of each and every participant along a very specific and clear-cut path, along the sides of which I suspect are erected walls topped with barbed wire. Ravitch says, "Before you set out on a journey, you have to know where you are going"(377). If the only purpose of the journey is the arrival, a great deal of experience is lost along the way. Robert Pirsig (1967) notes that it is the top of the mountain that defines the sides, but it is the sides of the mountain on which grows life. Unlike Ravitch's prescription for education, I hold that a journey ought to be a process of exploration and that to know where you are going would be to deny the activity itself for the distant product of arrival.

I believe education ought to be a willful and conscious getting lost so that we might have the opportunity of finding ourselves again. Education ought to be understood as the Thoravian saunter; we must leave home that we might know home everywhere. The walk to which I refer invites a willed sense of lostness and displacement from which new discovery and relationships are possible. To take a walk is to leave home, is commensurate with starting out on a life's journey, and therefore, for Thoreau, could only properly be undertaken when one was prepared never to return home again. I have never imagined that Thoreau truly meant that the walker must actually say goodbye to all that was familiar and never *physically* return; after all, Thoreau lived an entire life in the small town of Concord, Massachusetts, and stated more than once that there was world enough in Concord to consume the efforts of his days. Rather, Thoreau seems to suggest that the engagement in the experience of the walk would alter forever—if the walker was prepared—the manner in which the world would be perceived and in which it would be engaged. Indeed, during the walk one becomes a walker. I think this is the meaning of Thoreau's invitation: to take a walk was to engage in life, to engage in what Pinar and Grumet (1976, 1994) call *currere*. For Pinar curriculum is not the course about which the runner runs, it is not the path upon which the learner treads; rather, curriculum is the process of walking itself, the engagement in the activity of walking; curriculum is the verb *currere*. In walking one creates the path. In walking becomes the walker.

The traditional notion of home must be abandoned that we might know our home everywhere. Home functions as the controlling center from which emanate prescribed paths. Home is the place of originary interpellations, a term I understand to mean "to question and therefore to call into being."[4] I believe with Althusser (1971, 176) that "[Even] before its birth, the child is therefore always-already a subject, appointed as a subject in and by the specific familial ideological configuration in which it is 'expected' once it has been conceived." From the very beginning of our lives we are defined by others. Even the newborn, pediatricians T. Berry Brazleton and Bertram Cramer note (1990, 15), is "never a total stranger . . . We would call the

---

[4] Thoreau was originally named David Henry and later changed his name to Henry David.

child-to-be a transference object, that is, unconscious feelings and relationships of the parents will be transposed onto the child." We bring children into a society where they are marked from birth, tracked and traced and incapable of getting lost with the hope of finding oneself in self-(re)production. In the name of protection and safety, our children—much less ourselves—are rarely free from surveillance and are subject often to the definitions and pathways others have laid out. Walking, in the Thoravian sense, is frowned upon. And so we learn usually what others know; because we are rarely permitted to travel, we can rarely come to our own knowledge.

Even before their arrival in school, students are all objects of interpellations—products of the uninterrupted stream of writing that attributes to them a subjectivity that must then be maintained by that tie to home. We are discovered by our place along that path, and we are enthusiastically welcomed when we can make our way back to home. In that arrival we are who we are thought to be and have always been. "Home," says Warren, in Frost's (1967) canonical poem *Death of the Hired Hand*, "is the place where when you have to go there they have to take you in." Home is the ultimate refuge to which return is always possible. Except that in Bob Dylan's noncanonical cautionary tale, "The Ballad of Frankie Lee and Judas Priest," Frankie Lee finds himself not safe but trapped and threatened within the haven of Judas Priest's home. Enticed there by Judas Priest by the promise of warmth and safety, Frankie Lee discovers that he has "soon lost all control/Over everything that he had made/While the mission bells did toll" (Dylan 1966). Frankie Lee has forfeited his own life for the anticipated safety of home. And the "moral of this story," the narrator suggests, is "don't go mistaking Paradise/For that home across the road." Home may operate as the determining center, may function as the defining mechanism and promise endless return and permanent refuge. Home holds us to the conventional paths by an uninterrupted stream of writing, the many white pebbles we have been taught to drop, the practice and activity of the panopticonal mechanism by which we then are constrained to define ourselves. The curriculum emanates along the paths from home along which children move in diachronic regularity.

But to renounce home—the prescribed curriculum—that original centering device, is to free ourselves to become our own centers. "All things are up and down, east and west, to me," Thoreau (1962, 39) declares. "In me is the Forum out of which go the Appian and Sacred ways, and a thousand beside to the ends of the world." Wherever Thoreau is, that is where home begins. "Let us wander where we will, the universe is built round about us, and we are central still. If we look into the heavens they are concave, and if we were to look into a gulf as bottomless, it would be concave also" (Thoreau 1961, 414). Having recognized home within, there is no longer need for return, no center about which to revolve, no suns to hold us in our orbital place, no way to be but productively lost. "Having abandoned the reality of the center," Barthes tells us of the city of Tokyo, "the center [becomes] no longer anything but a frivolous idea, subsisting there not in order to broadcast power, but to give to [the city's] . . . urban movement the support for its empty central obliging the traffic in a perpetual departure from the normal path" (in Block 1989, 260). It is, I believe, in these perpetual departures that deny home that lostness may be experienced and learning may begin, and it is what the schools might promote by abandoning curricula already in place. "When you got nothing you got nothing to lose," Bob Dylan (1965) cries. "You're invisible now, you got no secrets to conceal./ How does it feel," he asks, "to be on your own/Like a complete unknown/Like a Rolling Stone?" Here invisibility broadcasts not absence, secrecy, or reclusiveness masking paranoia, but freedom and possibility. Here an acceptance of lostness does not offer direction but admits of the knowledge proclaimed by the Grateful Dead: "*If* I knew the way, I would take you home" (Garcia & Hunter 1971, emphasis added). We must all find our own way home by making home within.

To get lost—to leave home—is to abandon even the notion of the path. That path, created by the exercise of power that defines it and the traveler who treads upon it, determines direction, supervises the perspectives, and is responsible for controlling thought and action. Thoreau notes how quickly the single path he had worn to the pond for his morning ablutions supervised and determined the way and how he then knew he would have to leave Walden, for "I had other lives to live." Indeed, he complains, perhaps others had continued in his path after he had abandoned it. We must teach our children itinerancy that we might offer them the freedom of intellec-

tual vagabondage, at home nowhere yet everywhere, neither
determined nor produced by any path. "How many things con-
cur to keep a man at home, to prevent his yielding to his incli-
nation to wander. Man does not travel as easily as the birds
migrate. He is not everywhere at home, like flies" (Thoreau
1962, 245). Certainly contemporary schooling denies this sauntering, this walking. In the name of education we deny learning. It's alright, ma, I'm only bleeding.

At present, children arrive at school from home. Perhaps
we might consider that occasion of arrival as the outset of a
Thoravian walk. Of course, it is not now so conceived. It is in
schools that we presently intend to teach these children to enter the social world out of which the school has arisen. In the
metaphors we have developed here, we organize schools so that
children will learn to march rather than to take a walk. "School-
to-work transition" and national standards are today's educational buzz words. Schools are places where knowledge can be
gained but not produced, where children will be organized into
social members before they are asked to think of themselves as
identities part of a social community, where presence and
observability are requisite values. Children now enter from the
familial world into one both detached and familiar—detached
in that the care and nurture that many children derive from
home is denied in school, and familiar because the social values that the school represents and offers are those of the society from which children are delivered to school. In this manner, children are educated to enter a world prepared for them,
in which certain roles and positions are organized to receive
them, and the paths, roles, and positions are very carefully
defined. We should know, Ravitch reminds us, before we begin where it is we are going. Walking here is in lockstep and
requires neither risk- nor leave-taking. There is no movement,
however, without risk-taking and no growth unless it is by our
movement. Thoreau (1961, 367) declares triumphantly: "When
every other path would fail, with singular and unerring confidence we advance on our particular course. What risks we run!
famine and fire and pestilence, and the thousand forms of a
cruel fate,—and yet, every man lives till he—dies." Education
must be understood as the walking, but it cannot be defined
prior to the walk. "[My life] will cut its own channel like a

mountain stream, and by the longest ridge is not kept from the sea at last." The citizens of Thekla, in Italo Calvino's *Invisible Cities* (1974, 127), are continually constructing their city. A stranger passing through questions the citizens on their activity. He asks, "What meaning does your construction have? . . . What is the aim of a city under construction unless it is a city? Where is the plan you are following, the blueprint?" But the citizens are too busy to stop their work and show the stranger the plans by which they work. At nightfall, however, work stops in Thekla, and the stranger awaits the words of its citizens. They descend their ladders. They point to the heavens. "Darkness falls over the building site. The sky is filled with stars. 'There is the blueprint,' they say." The universe might be the pattern for our educational institutions, and there is no end or definitiveness to it.

Perhaps we might think of curriculum as the development of estrangement, as the deliberate effort of a walk. It is willful and voluntary; it is the production of experience that forever alters the future and the past. Our concern as curriculum developers must be with the unfolding of curriculum that promotes education as exploration and in which activity production is not only of an artistic creation but of the artist as well. As educators we must design means by which we might maintain communication with our students and yet permit them the freedom of the journey that we believe education must be. As teachers we must create conditions for the walk, afford students the opportunity to experience the sense of being lost, offer them development in practices of self-awareness, and establish means by which we might maintain communication with the traveler such that we do not impede the travel, that we facilitate yet monitor the walk, monitor but not direct the walk. Needless to say, though I will say it, there must be more to the walk than the walking.

Chapter VI

Walking, Curriculum, and Neuroscience

Walking sounds very much akin to the processes of education: self-conscious movement along a way by experiment, activity, and consideration in which change is constantly effected in the action. Neuroscientists are now suggesting that consciousness and learning are originally based in the activity of the body and may be understood as integrally founded in physiological processes; the movements and states of the body provide the content to the brain resulting in neural circuitries and patterns that will become mind. Dr. Antonio Damasio (1994, 90) declares that "having a mind means that an organism forms neural representations which can become images, be manipulated in a process called thought, and eventually influence behavior by helping predict the future, plan accordingly, and choose the next action." Learning entails the development of neural circuitries that are responsible for producing these neural representations: the function of the brain is to be "well informed about what goes on in the rest of the body, the body proper; about what goes on in itself; and about the environment surrounding the organism, so that suitable, survivable accommodations can be achieved between organism and environment" (Damasio 90). Thus, walking and education are, or at least ought to be, activities in which the process is of greater significance than the product. Indeed, the process seems to be all. The production of new neural representations—what will be referred to below as dispositional representations (Damasio 1994) or neuronal groups (Edelman 1992)—requires that the body be engaged in action or at least think it is so involved.[1]

---

[1] However, even precise simulations will not reproduce the exact conditions of reality.

Learning requires movement and sensory activity that may be accompanied by actual emotions (collection of changes in body state connected to particular mental images that have activated a specific brain system—the self) and feelings (the self-reflective *experience* of such changes in juxtaposition to the mental images that initiated the cycle of changes that comprise the event—the subject). It is the experience of emotions and feelings that facilitates and accompanies thinking. That is, subjectivity emerges when the brain produces not just images of an object (perception) nor images of an organism responding to objects (emotions), but the image of an organism perceiving and responding to an object (feelings). Thus, it would appear to me that the process of education, like the venture of walking, ought to make the familiar unfamiliar and the familial exotic so that experience might lead not only to new perceptions and new emotions but to the production of self in the awareness of these effects. Activity must be engaged in so as to produce the establishment of new circuitries—new recategorizations—based in the body states and the concurring images that are attached to those states. The student engaged in curriculum ought to experience the amazing grace of once being lost and being found again. These events might be understood as a physiological as well as an existential and phenomenological event.

It has been long accepted that education is a matter of teaching critical thinking, of developing lifelong learners, even of providing skills that would facilitate existence in the world.[2] With these objectives I have no qualms. Indeed, we would have our students be critically aware not only of themselves and their social construction but of their environments as well. But I would like to consider these achievements as a process steeped not solely in the cognitive but in the physiological as well. I want to suggest that this growth that we refer to as education is, in fact, only possible in an interaction that originates in body states and with the environment. I want to suggest that consciousness itself arises as a product of walking, is based in the activity of the body, and cannot exist without it. All learning

---

[2] Richard Paul (1990, 7) defines critical thinking as "thinking about your thinking while you're thinking in order to make your thinking better."

requires movement; without questions we seek no answers and need not venture out. Movement is a bodily experience: it involves images and emotions and feelings and results in learning. As Damasio (1994) notes, "If there had been no body, there would have been no brain." Learning is a psychosomatic event; to heed this process would require in the next century a drastic alteration in the structures of education.

Learning may be best conceptualized as walking. When engaged in schooling, the body should move through an environment, as it does in walking; and that bodily activity contributes a content to the brain that is inseparable from the workings of mind. From his transcendental heights Thoreau (1961, 126) says, "The mind never makes a great and successful effort without a corresponding energy of the body." From his understanding in neuroanatomy Antonio Damasio (1994, 111) says: "as we develop from infancy to adulthood, the design of brain circuitries that represent our evolving body and its interaction with the world seems to depend on the activities in which the organism engages, and on the action of innate bioregulatory circuitries, *as the latter react to such activities.*" When I walk my body moves through a specific physical environment. The condition of the body makes possible a particular mode of walking—as say, a result of gender, disability, race or ethnicity. Furthermore, the effort within the specific topography requires the body to react in a certain manner *depending on the environment and the requisite movement through it.* Finally, that movement depends on emotions based in prior learning, themselves the productions of neural circuitries. Consider Hansel and Gretel discussed earlier: the behavior of the two children in the story derives from their body states—hunger; from emotions which begin in body states—fear; from gender—Hansel is the leader; and from prior learning—Hansel had learned to drop pebbles to mark his path. Certainly, Thoreau's movement through his beloved woods, too, must be understood as deriving from body states, though I doubt he ever took to dropping little white pebbles to recover his path. Similarly, as the female visitor to New York City walks its streets at night, she carries her body in ways quite different from that of one of the city's lifelong male residents. Their bodily experiences produce not only a different city but different people in that city.

Knowledge is embodied in neural configurations that must be activated. Knowledge production consists in the neural firings (dispositional representations) in an attempt to replicate patterns that were once experienced. These potential patterns are contained in what Damasio (1994, 102-4) calls dispositional representations. Dispositional representations exist as

> potential patterns of neuron activity in small ensembles of neurons I call "convergence zones"; that is, they consist of a set of neuron firing dispositions within the ensemble. The dispositions related to recallable images were acquired through learning, and thus we can say they constitute a memory. . . . A dispositional representation is a dormant firing potentiality which comes to life when neurons fire, with a particular pattern, at certain rates, for a certain amount of time, and toward a particular target which happens to be another ensemble of neurons.

Learning is the development of dispositional representations. The process begins in the body. Movements of the body's effort within a specific environment produce certain *somatic* or *body states* (Damasio 1994, 173), and these states may then mark an image.

The marked image is a *somatic marker*. Somatic markers are feelings that mark a certain image with a body state such that reasoning may be better enhanced. The perception of a specific aroma produces a specific emotion that is then linked to a particular image. A somatic marker may be the smell of a certain scent or the sound of a known melody; nevertheless, the emotion begins in the body and the experience of that emotion produces the feeling: the somatic marker. Walter Freeman (1991), too, suggests that nerve cell assemblies are a product of learning and that once formed are capable of generalizing that learning based on little stimuli. Freeman (1991, 82) notes that receptors in various areas of the recepting organ—say the nose—may be stimulated and yet the brain recognizes as a result of learning that all the separate and disparate messages refer to the same stimulus—say, the odor of the perfume:

> If we are correct, the existence of a nerve cell assembly would help explain both the foreground-background problem and generalization over equivalence reports. In the first instance, the assembly would confer "front-runner" status on stimuli that experience, stored in the Hebbian synapses, has made important to the individual. In the sec-

ond instance, the assembly would ensure that information from any subset of receptors, regardless of where in the nose they were located, would spread immediately over the entire assembly and from there to the rest of the bulb.

Somatic markers, the connection between body state and image, represent a specific instance of feelings and are a function of learning. Somatic markers facilitate reflective action. "[M]ost somatic markers we use for rational decision-making probably were created in our brains during the process of education and socialization, *by connecting specific classes of stimuli with specific classes of somatic state*" (Damasio 1994, 177, emphasis added). The efficacy of somatic markers is that they facilitate the "connection of certain emotions and feelings to predicted future outcomes of certain scenarios" (Damasio 1994, 173-74) such that certain options are opened and certain options are closed for future action. These feelings and emotions are tied to body states and connected to certain images. I do not eat peaches because of a severe episode of nausea that occurred when taking certain medication while eating the fruit, and which forever became associated with vomiting. Thoreau throws away a handsome paperweight given him at Walden Pond because the *physical effort* required to dust it is *emotionally* aversive to him. The aversion (feeling) to numbers from which I suffer derives in part from the unpleasant physical experience of high school mathematics classes in which I sat for much of the time confused. I once received a zero on a fourth retest in a physics class because it was comprised of four math problems. The teacher called my home to report my failure. It's alright, ma, I'm only bleeding.

Somatic markers are, as the name suggests, based in the body but are what can also be referred to as qualia, or phenomenological experience. Gerald Edelman (1992, 136) says that "Qualia, individual to each of us, are recategorizations by higher-order consciousness of value-laden perceptual relations in each sensory modality or their conceptual combinations with each other. We report them crudely to others; they are more directly reportable to ourselves." Qualia derive from the monitoring of the body's experience "*while* thoughts about specific contents roll by" (Damasio 1994, 145, emphasis in original). Qualia are the conceptual and reconceptual organization of experience. They represent the way things *feel*; Damasio suggests that feelings "are first and foremost about the body . . . they offer us the *cognition of our visceral and musculoskeletal state* as it becomes affected by preorganized mechanisms and by the cognitive structures which we have developed under their influence" (159). In other words, the perception of qualia, what Edelman (1992, 114) defines as "the collection of personal or subjective experiences, feelings, and sensations that accompany awareness,"[3] represents the individual's generation of connections; these connections may be the subject of narrative and best understood to ourselves. Because qualia can only be individually experienced, they can only be coarsely narrated to others. "An individual can report his or her experience to an observer, but that report must always be partial, imprecise, and relative to his or her own personal context" (Edelman 114). Qualia are the articulations of somatic markers.

These qualia are based immediately in the body. Positive body states incline us toward a certain possibility of decisions and negative body states make certain decisions aversive. The expectations of companionship send me out into the bars; the experience of the empty barstools sends me home again. As I write these sentences—as I think—the neural circuitries that make possible the production of these words make me happy and increase the generation and variety of images that make reasoning efficient. I continue to write. And so on. When the writing goes badly, I feel unhappy and the generation of words and ideas slows down. I do not continue to write. I grow more depressed. And so on. Negative body states tend to be accompanied by a slower generation of images with less diversity and inefficient reasoning. "[B]ecause both the signal of the body state (positive or negative) and the style and efficiency of cognitions were triggered from the same system, they tend to be concordant" (Damasio 1994, 147). That is, my happiness or sadness may be defined as the perception of a particular body state juxtaposed with certain images and complemented by a certain cognitive style. Mind is given content by the body. "Somatic markers are thus acquired by experience, under the con-

---

[3] This is the subject of Robert Pirsig's *Zen and the Art of Motorcycle Maintenance* (1967).

trol of an internal preference system and under the influence of an external set of circumstances which include not only entities and events with which the organism must interact, but also social conventions and ethical rules" (Damasio 179). Descartes' *cogito* must be understood as derived in such relations. Later symbolic systems may articulate that state and image—imperfectly as we now understand—but we acknowledge that reasoning is situated first in the body. The body numbed denies learning or restricts the organism's capacity for it. It's alright, ma, I'm only bleeding.

Phenomenologically, in the walking one's point of view is in constant transition; each step calls into question the safety of present positions. Life itself understood as a walk is a type of experiment, and each step is undertaken with the expectation that the future will not be the past. In this experience that I have called walking, one's way cannot be known before stepping out. It is all hypothesis; lostness is implicit in activity. Learning—the development of somatic markers—is implicit in the process. William Pinar (1994) notes that life itself is by all accounts a profound experiment and therefore might be understood as equivalent to the process of education. It would seem that what we have learned from neurophysiology demands that we understand education as that process by which brain circuitries develop by the interaction of environment and genome and by which the categorization of those circuitries on a background of value result in adaptive changes in behavior that satisfy value (Edelman 1992, 118). Value may be understood finally as that which promotes survival. Values produce qualia.

On Reason

Value is set both intrinsically by the human genome—perhaps we might say that the genome establishes constraints[4]—and in interaction with the particular environment. And value is di-

---

[4] I would love to be capable of flapping my arms to fly. Alas, the human genome constrains me. But the experience of flying in an airplane affords me some sense of what the earth looks like from the sky. The invariances I acknowledge as self, however, recognize that it is not I who is flying. I know what the earth looks like from the air, but I also do not know what the earth looks like to a bird flying in the air.

rected toward the organism's survival. We may call such cognitive processes steeped in values reasoning: "It is perhaps accurate to say that the purpose of reasoning is deciding and that the essence of deciding is selecting a response option, that is, choosing a nonverbal action, a word, a sentence, or some combination thereof, among the many possible at the moment, in connection with a given situation" (Damasio 1994, 165). Reasoning then, is a brain function we call mind that both results from and results in the production of neural circuitries that organize experience and thought based on value. The neural circuitires are themselves the production of physical interaction of the organism in the environment. Edelman (1992, 109) declares that conceptual learning occurs when "Structures in the brain, instead of categorizing outside inputs from sensory modalities, categorize parts of past global mappings according to modality, the presence or absence of movement, and the presence or absence of relationships between perceptual categorization." As compared to the idea of the homunculus sitting centrally somewhere in the brain organizing images, this view recognizes the complex and parallel neural firings in different brain locations that produce consciousness. Daniel Dennett (1991, 135) asks, "Where does it all come together?" Answering his own question he responds, "Nowhere." Consciousness arises from a subtle, complex integration of multiple maps from separate places in the brain. This organization produces what is called "global mapping," defined as (Edelman 1992, 118):

> a dynamic structure containing multiple reentrant local maps (both motor and sensory) that are able to interact with nonmapped parts of the brain (the hippocampus, the basal ganglia and the cerebellum). Global mapping permits sectional events to be joined to the organism's behavior and motor activity. In such a manner a "scene" might be produced, a scene now defined as "a spatiotemporally ordered set of categorizations of familiar and nonfamiliar events, *some with and some without necessary physical or causal connections to others in the same scene.*"

In such a way, an event gathers consequence not only as a result of its position and energy in the physical world but as a result of the relative value the event has been accorded as a result of prior learning—of the organization of prior global mapping structures.

Higher order consciousness, conceptual learning, is the production of maps of maps: "Consciousness rises from a special set of relationships between perception, concept formation and memory. These psychological functions depend on categorization mechanisms in the brain . . . memory is influenced by evolutionarily established value systems and by homeostatic control systems characteristic of each species" (Edelman 1992, 149). Value comes, so to speak, *as* the territory rather than *with* it. What the environment might provide is often what we expect to be available in and from it. "Value," Robert Pirsig (1967, 277) notes, "is the predecessor of structure. It's the preintellectual awareness that gives rise to it. Our structured reality is preselected on the basis of value, and really to understand structured reality requires an understanding of the value source from which it's derived." Perception, J. J. Gibson (1979) argues, is not a response to an environment; rather, perception is an act of information pickup and is selective rather than instructional. Information is anything that helps the human organism reduce alternatives (see Smith 1988) for decision making. Higher order consciousness, then, results from the activity of the brain creating maps of itself using symbolic memories.

This capacity seems to be specialized in human organisms. Animals may connect two kinds of categorization and may engage in conceptual categorization,[5] but they cannot do so in reference to a symbolic memory. There may be no past self in the scene but, rather, a present that is produced in memory. The organization of a past and future is integrally dependent on the concept of the self that arises through symbolic memories.

Now we do not define this reasoning as the body's response; reason is not physical. Rather, these somatic markers based in the body help reduce the alternatives that facilitate reason.

---

[5] For example, an animal may enter an environment and know it is in danger based on a "categorization occurring on a background of value to result in adaptive changes in behavior that satisfy value." However, as I have said, the animal lacks the ability to be "aware of that memory or plan an extended future for itself based on that memory" (Edelman 1992, 122). The animal does not seem to be able to produce its self in that scene in the past.

Indeed, it is a child's unconcern of body that makes possible the risk taking that horrifies the adult.[6] My decision to study for a test is founded first in the body feeling experienced when the thought of failing the test is considered. That body state may then be linked (linguistically) to feeling states of fear or shame or ambition or rebellion; or it may be linked to images of parents, significant others, and friends. Indeed, the psychoanalytic transference that has great relevance in the classroom is founded upon such a linkage. My gut feeling is exactly that: a somatic state that affects my reasoning. Indeed, my reasoning is severely altered without that gut feeling, as Damasio discusses in his essay on Phineas Gage and patient "Elliot." That gut feeling derives from the body and is a powerful influence on reasoning; "Feelings do seem to depend on a dedicated multi-component system that is indissociable from biological regulation" (Damasio 1994, 245). To ignore this complex relationship would lead to social systems such as the schools that deny the human organism.

Many critical somatic markers occur during childhood, as I have suggested in an earlier chapter. But somatic markers continue to develop throughout life and certainly arise during the process we may understand as education. William Pinar (1975, 371) accuses the schools of denying the body: "The discomfort of school furniture results in a diminution of physical feeling. One simply cannot tolerate physical discomfort hour after hour, day after day, year after year without suppressing such discomfort. One necessarily loses much of one's ability to experience tactile sensations. One becomes numb." I have not noticed a drastic change in school furniture in the twenty-five years of my life in schools. Damasio cautions that the overabundance of violence in "real life, newscasts or audiovisual fiction" may be reducing the value of emotions and feelings in producing social behavior by desensitizing such action. The types of somatic markers are clearly determined by the specific engagement in types of educative activities. The body states experienced by Descartes sitting in his armchair are radically different

---

[6] See Francois Truffaut's film *Small Change* for a wonderful representation of this. In a central scene a young child playfully cavorts on the edge of a window several stories high while adults in the film and audience sit panicked.

from those experienced by Thoreau actively engaged in the walk. The two men also knew different things. Children raised in war zones know different things than, say, most middle-class Americans. The awareness of body states—and Descartes was simply unconcerned with his perhaps because he sat in so comfortable an armchair[7]—and the capacity to link those states via symbolic systems to an organism in the past and the future produces self. "At each moment," Damasio (1994, 240) declares, "the state of self is constructed, from the group up. It is an evanescent reference state, so continuously and consistently *re*constructed that the owner never knows it is being *re*made unless something goes wrong with the remaking." The process to which I refer as subjectivity—self-reflective consciousness—begins, as I suggest, in the body . . . the body engaged in a walk.

The Body and the Self

The result of the complex workings of mind based in the body is what is romantically referred to as "the self." That self is, in the words of neuroscientist Antonio Damasio (1994, 227), "a repeatedly reconstructed biological state." In the walking becomes the walker. Education based in the body is consistent with evolution (Damasio 229):

> Developing a mind, which really means developing representations of which one can be conscious as images, gave organisms a new way to adapt to circumstances of the environment that could not have been foreseen in the genome. The basis for that adaptability probably began by constructing images of the body proper in operation, namely images of the body as it responded to the environment externally (say, using a limb) and internally (regulating the viscera).

Damasio claims that the self is finally the image an organism has in the act of perceiving and responding to an object. This

---

[7] Descartes says that "From that I knew that I was a substance, the whole essence or nature of which is to think, and that for its existence there is no need of any place, nor does it depend on any material thing; so that this 'me,' that is to say, the soul by which I am what I am, is entirely distinct from body, and is even more easy to know than is the latter; and even if the body were not, the soul would not cease to be what it is" (in Damasio 1994, 249).

is very similar to the idea of the self posited by psychotherapist Christopher Bollas, who notes that he has "hundreds, thousands, by my death millions, of sequential self states arising
from the dialectical meetings between my self and the object
world, which release me to some conscious knowing of my life"
(Bollas 1992, 29). The self is not unitary but multiplex, and
different selves may be evoked in specific interactions with the
environment, which is never the same. Perhaps it is for this
reason that Thoreau tells us that although he walks every day
in his immediate vicinity, he has never yet exhausted the opportunities. The availability of objects is unending and unpredictable. What is requisite is that his body be active and engaged in the walk—that he interact with objects.

The activity of the walk is one defined by the interdepen-
dence of the physical upon the mental such that either is known
through its situation in the other. Thoreau (1980, 99) notes
that "it sometimes happens that I cannot easily shake off the
village. The thought of some work will run in my head and I
am not where my body is,—I am out of my senses." Though the
walker is physically engaged, there is no education here. Neuroscientist Antonio Damasio (1994, xvii) declares: "The physiological operations that we call mind are derived from the structural and functional ensemble [of body and brain together]
rather than from the [operations of] brain alone: mental phenomena can be fully understood only in the context of an
organism's interacting in the environment." Walking, then,
more than a physical activity, and not at all like Descartes' mis-
taken belief that he could create himself seated complacently
in his armchair and from within his mind alone, acknowledges
a self-aware and physical engagement of the organism with the
environment such that the walker and world are produced in
the activity itself. During this walk the ideas of chance and
accident are as intrinsically important as direction and purpose; the brain's development is contingent upon the body's
situation in the physical conditions. The precise arrangement
of systems and circuits in the brain, out of which mind arises,
comes about under *"the influence of environmental circumstances
[no two brains are alike, even between identical twins] complemented
and constrained by the influence of the innately and precisely set
circuits concerned with biological regulation"* (Damasio 1994, 110,

emphasis in original). The mind, as it arises out of the content of the body states, then, might only be understood as the product of interaction between the biological organism and the environment; the self, the self-aware organism, can be known as the process of that interaction. My distaste for calamari is based in the queasiness I experience in the body regarding the texture, consistency, and even source of the delicacy. Similarly, my aversion to Nazis is a complex response that is based in the body state. Dennett (1991) declares that the self is merely the center of narrative gravity, the fictional unified agent about whom all the words and images refer and from which they emanate. Those images are based in a bodystate: the loss of a sense of body, as in anosognosia, could endanger the survival of the organism. The body situates itself in the world to maximize its pleasure (its survival) and that situation "prepare[s] the ground for conscious, cognitive processing" (Damasio 1994, 222). As I stand on the ground looking up at the Steeplechase Ride at Coney Island, it is with my body that the first response to the invitation to ride occurs.

Indeed, it seems to be true that the actual development of the brain is a product of the interaction between the brain and the environment. Neuroscientists attest that the structure of the brain out of which mind arises is determined not only by its precise structure, the human genome, but also by individual activity and circumstances and the self-organizing pressures required by the complexity of the system. Walking moves the body through an environment where interaction between the design of brain circuitries that represent our evolving body and the world occurs. Thus, the complex neural circuitry that comprise brain design "seems to depend on the activities in which the organism engages, and on the action of innate bioregulatory circuitries, *as the latter react to such activities*" (Damasio 1994, 111, emphasis in original). The human genome, then, is significant in the individual's development but is not determining.[8] Activity is, on the other hand, a necessary though

---

[8] It is, of course, this condition that makes education possible and that makes absurd the claims of such charlatans as Charles Murray and Richard Herrnstein-Smith (1994) that intelligence is a fixed inheritable quantity.

not sufficient cause of development. Thus, the unpredictable experiences in which an individual engages in the walk do have influence upon the design of brain circuitries both directly and indirectly "via the reaction it sets off in the innate circuitries, and the consequences that such reactions have in the overall process of circuit shaping" (Damasio 1994, 112). Were the activity of the walk habituating, little would change in brain circuitries and learning would not occur. There is, it appears, more to the walk than the walking.

What neuroscientists explain as mind from a perspective founded in biology, social scientists address from the viewpoint of psychology. As the neuroscientists understand mind as a product of the development and organization of neural circuitries from which will arise the capacity to produce images, so from a psychological point of view self might be understood as a process of organization of the invariant pattern of awarenesses of the subjective experience that will later come to be called the self. For phenomenologists the activity of bracketing attempts to define those invariances that represent the core self. Object relations theorists suggest that the self results from interaction with objects in the environment, acknowledging that if there is a core self, it can only be known through its mediation with objects. Nonetheless, a physiological basis for mind and for the self that is often equated with mind is accepted. Daniel Stern (1985) focuses on the physical action of infants in their environment and their responses to that action as the means for establishing invariances. Stern says that infants are predisposed (as a function of the human genome) to be aware of self-organizing processes—of what can be called the "me" and what is the "not-me." Stern's research suggests that the union with another which is mythologized in certain psychological circles is, in fact, only possible **after** the sense of core self and other exists, that self develops from activity, and that there is never a time when there is not a self/other differentiation. Relationship follows from individuation rather than vice versa, but individuation develops from interactions with the environment. Aggression, as Winnicott (1984) defines it, is not a response to an impinging environment (a response to frustration) but a reaching out toward it. For Winnicott, aggression is the infant's natural venturing into contact with the world. Its developing self requires a facilitating environment. Thus, neurologically and psychologically, self may be explained as arising as a result of action.

Indeed, the psychological development of the individual can only be explained by the physiological organization of the individual—the development of neural circuitries under the pressure of environmental interaction with the brain's structures. Infant psychiatrist Daniel Stern (1985, 7) defines self as the

> invariant pattern of awarenesses that arise only on the occasion of the infant's actions or mental processes. An invariant pattern of awareness is a form of organization. It is the organizing subjective experience of whatever it is that will later be verbally referenced as the "self." This organizing subjective experience is the preverbal, existential counterpart of the objectifiable, self-reflective, verbalizable self.

In Stern's view, the infant's developing sense of self arises through action and reflection upon that action, defined in this preverbal existential time as the realization of invariant awarenesses: the awareness of what does not change. Neurophysiologically, these invariances may be defined as "the product of brain maps independently receiving signals either from the outside world or from other brain maps and forming through reentrant signaling active combinations of neuronal groups in one map to different combinations in the other map" (Edelman 1992, 87). Maps, Edelman (89) says, are neural circuitries in the brain that relate points on the two-dimensional receptor sheets of the body (such as the skin or the retina of the eye) to corresponding points on the sheets making up the brain. These maps coordinate inputs and effect categorization of experience: it would appear that it is done in good part by checking for invariances.

> To explain how categorization may occur, we can use the workings of what I have called a "classification couple" in the brain. This is a minimal unit consisting of two functionally different maps made up of neuronal groups and connected by reentry. Each map *independently* receives signals from other brain maps or from the world. . . . Within a certain time period, reentrant signaling strongly connects certain active combinations of neuronal groups in one map to different combinations in the other map . . . In this way the functions and activities in one map are connected and correlated with those in another map (Edelman 1992, 87).

Thus a phenomenological perspective on self is founded on a physiological basis and is provided its content from it. Maps result in concept formation that permits the organism to connect one perceptual categorization to another in the absence of the original stimuli that triggered those categorizations. I can recall the home I lived in when I was a child although it has been razed long since; I can see my fourth grade teacher although she has long since died; I can even feel her classroom. The formation of these maps depends quite sensitively on "place (which other cells are around), time (when one event occurs in relation to another), and correlated activity (whether cells fire together or change together chemically over a period of time)" (Edelman 1992, 22). These contingencies derive from the interaction of the organism within the environment constrained by the genome. Reentry is the linking of maps that have been experientially formed. "A fundamental premise [of the theory of neuronal group selection] is that the selective coordination of the complex patterns of interconnection between neuronal groups by reentry is the basis of behavior. Indeed, reentry (combined with memory . . .) is the main basis for a bridge between physiology and psychology" (Edelman 1992, 83). Reentrant connections might be understood as recursive connectivity among and between neuronal cell groups and extrinsic inputs from the environment.[9] Gerald Edelman, explaining the physiological basis of psychological existence, has postulated the theory of neuronal group selection (TNGS) to account for the assumption "that all cognition and all conscious experience rest solely on processes and orderings occurring in the physical world" (82). His theory connects psychology and physiology by suggesting that brain maps (what Damasio refers to as dispositional representations; see above) interact by a process called reentry. These maps are configurations of neuronal groups that are the minimum unit for organizing behavior of

---

[9] One important aspect of this theory concerns the idea that the unit of selection in the brain—the unit that is primarily responsible for behavior—is the neuronal group and not the individual cell. This is important when we consider that neuronal groups—groups of nerve cells formed by activity in concert with the genome and based in value—although constrained in forming are not determined and are dependent on activity of the organism.

which thought must be considered a category (Edelman 1992, 87):

> . . . no individual neuron is selected in isolation; no individual neuron in a map reenters to only one other neuron in another map; and no individual neuron has the properties alone that it shows in a group.

In the production of neuronal groups and reentrant mappings, the organism, within limits set by the human genome, effects categorizations. That is, concept formation might be understood as constrained by the genetic composition of the organism but is ecologically based. Thus, the formation of the circuitry of the brain is organized by the human genome but only in interaction with an environment. Mind is a function of brain. That selection of coordinating neuronal groups and the resulting pattern of reentrant connections comes as a result of the organism's interaction in the environment. In the walking becomes the walker.

Reflection and the Body

I have said that subjectivity—selfhood—arises out of the organism's ability to perceive and respond to an object and to be aware of its response—to understand itself (and its dreams) as objects and to have the capacity and ability to use those objects. This process may be understood in the Deweyan (1991, 6, emphasis in original) concept of reflection: *"Active, persistent, and careful consideration of any belief or supposed form of knowledge in the light of the grounds that support it, and the further conclusions to which it tends,* constitutes reflective thought." I think that central to the idea of the walk is the process of reflection, an action upon which the walk seems to be premised and for which it is apparently designed. It is true that all walking produces some educational benefit, but it is the Thoravian walk that promotes the lostness which demands reflective thought. Hansel and Gretel's following the white pebbles along a prescribed path required no reflective thought. Without the capacity for reflection, we are merely ensnared in what Edelman (1992) calls primary consciousness, or the remembered present. This remembered present permits recognition but does not involve personal representation in that recognition. It is as if we have moved into an environment with which we are familiar—in which a specific emotion might be experienced—but have no sense of when we were ever in that environment before or even what happened there, although we recognize the environment. This may be an explanation of the experience of déjà vu. Primary consciousness constrains the individual to be mindful but mired in the present. Primary consciousness may depend on long-term memory, but in the absence of the capacity to engage in symbolization—to invest self in something that is not-self—the past cannot exist. "Where there is thought, things present act as signs or tokens of things not yet experienced. A thinking being can, accordingly, *act on the basis of the absent and the future*" (Dewey 1991; 14, emphasis in original). And without that memory, neither can self exist. The Thoravian walker must have the capacity to engage in reflection that the self lost may find itself again. That capacity depends on the engagement in symbolic systems. These systems are cultural capital and must be learned. Thoreau wrote at the least millions of words in his journal as he recorded his experiences. Out of those words he created other works.

The walk that is educational is that which begins in the expectation of lostness and the anticipation of being found. These expectations are based in a continuing self and therefore a status in a past and future. "In my walk I would fain return to my senses," says Thoreau (1980, 99). In this statement Thoreau announces a desire for a willed lostness that he might find himself again. The statement is also an acknowledgment of a self in a past and a future and of a recognizable transformation in that self. These findings are in fact acts of self-creation as a product of a reflective consciousness. I think that Thoreau means in this statement that the activity of mind and body must be attuned in the engagement of the walk and that the engagement in the physical activity of the walk should be accompanied by a consciousness of the experience of the walk and the walker in the experience. Walking should be play. That is, in the activity of the walk the self engages in activity—in experience with objects including the self as object—upon which it may reflect. "In play the subject releases the idiom of himself to the field of objects, where he is then transformed by the structure of that experience, and will bear the history of that encounter in the unconscious. . . . Each entry into an experience of an object is rather like being born again, as subjectivity is newly informed by the encounter, its history altered by a radically effective present that will change its structure" (Bollas 1992, 59). The "I" appears on the scene when that history is written—when the experience is defined *as* experience. This is the work of reflection and ought to be the substance of education. It is education to pursue the histories of our encounters: to know where we have been and what we have experienced. Dewey (1991, 15) says that "it is in virtue of the capacity of thought that given things are significant of absent things." We must become cognizant of the available objects as the mediums of such expression: memory becomes then "a gathering of internal objects, developing an inner constellation of feelings, ideas, part images, body positions, somatic registrations, and so forth that nucleate into a sustained inner form" (Bollas 1992, 59). Memory, as we have suggested, is also based in the physical.

Reflection, a characteristic of memory, is embedded in physiological processes. Gerald Edelman (1992) says that because memory is a property of the system and not a system itself it is, therefore, dynamic. Defining memory as the "specific enhancement of a previously established ability to categorize," Edelman notes that since perceptual categories are not immutable, they may be altered by the ongoing behavior of the animal. Memory results from continual recategorization, which arises as a result of the walking. "Because of new associations arising in these contexts, because of changing inputs and stimuli, and because different combinations of neuronal groups can give rise to a similar output, a given categorical response in memory may be achieved in several ways" (Edelman 1992, 102). Reflection may be understood as the active and conscious development of dispositional representations or global mappings. What memory and reflection may produce is the subject. The subject must first be engaged in walking.

Reflective thought, according to this view, is a matter of making connections, or at least the possibility of connection, between the object that is actually perceived and the object that is suggested.[10] That connection is steeped in both senses

---

[10] Perception is a conscious act stemming from prior experience, not an involuntary or indiscriminate reaction to the environment.

of the term physical: on the one hand, the connection is with and between objects; but on the other hand, the connection is based in neurophysiology. Edelman notes (1992, 149) that "as a selective system, the brain (especially the cerebral cortex) is a correlator. It correlates temporal inputs during its own development, and it correlates the properties of signals and scenes in its adult functioning to give rise to consciousness." With the development of the capacity to employ symbolic systems, it is possible that the brain may treat the symbols and their images and references as an independent world to be further categorized. This is accomplished by further connections between neuronal groups. The result is what is termed thinking: a construction of artificial objects that are entirely mental (Edelman 151), hence the invention of the unicorn, paranoia, mathematics, history, fiction, etc. But since thinking is then a product not of logic but of synthesized patterns based in education, it would seem impossible physiologically to determine meanings as is so often the case in educational matters. Meaning is a product of thought.

"Thought," says John Dewey (1991,14), "affords the sole method of escape from purely impulsive or purely routine action." Thought releases us from the remembered present. It does so by connecting things seen to things unseen—to an investment in the past and the future. From a more phenomenological perspective, Dewey suggests, "The thing [perceived] is regarded as in some way *the ground or basis of belief* in the suggested thing; it possesses the quality of evidence." Based in semiotic practice, the thing is not a thing of nothing;[11] rather, that thing is important not only for what it might be but also for what it might suggest, for the meanings a meaner might produce from it or with it. Meaning making is a decision-making process, but it is a cognitive process that is supplied content by the body. "In one sense," says Gibson (1979, 7), "the surroundings of a single animal are the same as the surroundings of all animals but . . . in another sense the surroundings of a single animal are different from those of any other animal." Meanings, of course, must be recognized as only partly

---

[11] I am reminded of Lear's tragic belief that "Nothing will come of nothing."

hegemonic; they can never be predetermined in large part because they are based in physiology. Edelman (1992, 25) acknowledges that "although the connectivity of neuronal systems in the central nervous system (particularly those that are mapped) is more or less similar from individual to individual, it is not identical." This connectivity depends on the interactions of the organism with the environment. In the walking becomes the walker.

Meanings are context-dependent and although constrained are highly individualized. This meaning-making process may be understood as based in the body. "Meaning," says Gerald Edelman (1992, 170), "takes shape in terms of concepts that depend on categorizations based on value. [Meaning] grows with the history of remembered body sensations and mental images. The mixture of events is individual, and in large measure, unpredictable." But these meanings exist not simply in the realm of pure thought, although it might appear that they do. This was, of course, Descartes' thesis: that he could create everything within the mind alone. It is only when thoughts are embodied in symbolic objects that it would *appear* that there is a realm of Platonic idealism. Contrary to Descartes, we must acknowledge that a necessary, though not sufficient, basis of thought resides in biology. When we establish thought on the basis of physiology, we refute the Platonic idealism that continues to permeate Western thought and education. I am suggesting that thoughts arise from complex "parallel, fluctuating, temporal processes of perception, concept formation, memory, and attentional states" (Edelman 1992, 174) activated and organized by the brain upon sensory information from the body itself that is itself organized by the brain. These thoughts may be then stored in a particular and personal symbolic object, be it a book, an art work, an automobile, or a flower. My weed is someone else's flower; my junk someone else's valuables. Meaning arises from the self-aware recognition of the self in the symbol—of the self's investment in the particular object that then becomes a symbol. Evocation of the self by objects derives from feelings that are based in somatic markers. Objects enable us to express ourselves, and once an object is used it may evoke the self in any combination of six orders: sensationally, structurally, conceptually, symbolically, mnemonically, or projectively. Each of these orders must be understood as embedded in meaning; meaning derives from categorization mechanisms, working through global mappings that involve our bodies and our personal histories.

Thinking, then, requires more than mere experience in the world, but it must be first based in worldly experience. Release from the immediacy of experience—from primary consciousness—requires engagement in symbolic systems; it requires, Edelman (1992, 174) declares, "social, affective and linguistic interactions. Thoughts, concepts, and beliefs are only individuated by reference to events in the outside world and by reference to social interactions with others, particularly those involving linguistic experience." The activities in which a person engages, the environments in which an organism interacts, have influence on what thoughts may arise and the signifiers that may then become signs. The availability of object experience is both product and process of education. And the activities in which the organism engages not only affect development of anatomy with regard to neural circuitries but are equally constrained by anatomy. Despite desire, I cannot flap my arms and fly. However, in the walking I engage in movement, and movement makes possible environmental changes that make learning imaginable. The interaction between brain and body produces mind. Hence, I might be able "to see" the world from the bird's-eye view by climbing a tree, by scaling a mountain, or by flying in an airplane.

As I have said, the walk to which I refer here is undertaken only when the old is to be made new, when the past is to be (re)considered and the future conceptualized. Thoreau's walks were always deliberate; the walking to which I refer is intentional and its proceeding will offer the meaner the opportunity to make new connections between the thing perceived (itself a product of learning) and the thing suggested. In other words, walking in the sense I am using it here is premised on the development of a self-aware organism; that is, one whose mind is, in the process of walking and from the development of symbolic systems from which concepts of self may be situated and articulated, engaged in the capacity for reflection. In neurophysiological terms, reflection might be understood as the development of circuitries whose organization and com-

plexities are such that the brain monitors not only its own activities but also those of the body state juxtaposed with the
image accompanying that body state. Indeed, the image may
even, as a result of prior learning, precede that state. Hence
arise, I believe, fears and promises that organize experience in
the world. Reflection here seems to refer to the brain's capacity to construct mechanisms[12] through experience "under the
control of an internal preference system [values] and under
the influence of an external set of circumstances which include
not only entities and events with which the organism must interact, but also social conventions and ethical rules" (Damasio
1994, 179). What issues as a result of this construction is narrative. Jerome Bruner (1990) argues for the centrality of the
construction of narrative in the development of sense of self.
Daniel Dennett (1991, 135) notes that consciousness might be
understood as a particular draft of a continually active and
developing narrative and that the self might be considered the
center of narrative gravity: "As soon as any such discrimination [say of color, tone, size, etc.] has been accomplished, [that
discrimination] becomes available for eliciting some behavior
. . . or for modulating some internal informational state." In
such a way the brain is continuously constructing a draft of
what state the body may be in or may move toward. These dis-
criminations are sensory; they result from moving the body in
a certain pattern to elicit pleasure. The drafts are the substance
of consciousness: in his multiple drafts theory of consciousness, I think Dennett suggests that the complex multitrack process of discrimination with its various editings, emendations,
incorporations, and overwritings, driven not only by the internal mechanisms that have developed evolutionarily to assure
survival, but by learned selections, may "yield, over the course
of time something *rather like* a narrative stream or sequence,
which can be thought of as subject to continual editing by many
processes distributed around in the brain, and continuing indefinitely into the future" (Dennett 1991, 135). Remembering
that perception is not instructional but selectional, we can

---

[12] As I have said above, Antonio Damasio refers to these mechanisms as
dispositional representations; Gerald Edelman calls them reentrant groups.

understand that reflection is the quintessential learning event. Reflection is awareness of the narrative stream by an agency that can identify itself as the substance of that stream. We may make inquiry into the stream at any time by the movement or anticipated movement of the body as a result of the gestalt. It is not a matter of stepping into the same stream twice: there is no homunculus (or central meaner) who can so venture. Rather, it is the movement of the stream that defines it and that gives it reality at any moment. Schooling that denies the possibility of walking precludes the possibility of thought. The basis is the body. It's alright, ma, I'm only bleeding.

When I'm on My Journey Don't You Weep after Me

Movement in the world is a constant interplay between what Frank Smith (1988) refers to as global and focal predictions. Movement is based in the body and its feelings. We anticipate our future on large scales—days, months, and years—we also anticipate our futures on very small scales, in steps and in minutes. The future is always the concern of the present; indeed, the future may constitute our very notion of the present. The reflective organism must always be more interested in where it will be next than in where it might be now and must therefore be actively probing the narrative stream for data based in the anticipation of the future. As I have said, *the images that comprise the stream are derived in content from the body and its state.* Our knowledge and our production of it derives from the mind's foundation in the body and the mind's influence upon that body. Again I repeat: this is no mere walking; though the way is strenuous it must be done in leisure and requires an effort that is neither exclusively physical nor singularly mental.

Now it seems to me that these processes of reflection, which are explicitly and implicitly integral to experiment, to education, and hence to life, and which since Descartes have been understood exclusively as being phenomenologically and cognitively based, are not independent of brain structures that are themselves physiologically situated. Thought, as it turns out, in and of itself cannot occur without a body; without a body there would be no mind. In neurophysiological terms, the interaction between brain circuits and the environment have influence on the brain circuitries and therefore on the development of the individual. As Damasio declares (1994, 110):

> The equivalent of the specifics that genes help set in the circuitry of the brain stem or hypothalamus comes to the remainder of the brain long after birth, as an individual develops through infancy, childhood, and adolescence, and as that individual interacts with the physical environment and other individuals. In all likelihood, as far as evolutionarily modern brain sectors are concerned, the genome helps set a general rather than a precise arrangement of systems and circuits. . . . [This precise arrangement] comes about under *the influence of environmental circumstances complemented and constrained by the influence of the innately and precisely set circuits concerned with biological regulation* [emphasis in original].

Here, phenomenology meets physiology: psychology and physiology are interwoven and mutually dependent. In the experience of the walk, the walker's brain monitors the state of the body that, in basic terms, is oriented to survival, and the brain does so in relation to the various triggers and subsequent evaluative images that produced the body state. Cognitive modes and activity grow out of emotions and feelings that have direct influence on the generation of further images that ultimately permit further discriminative states in an ongoing recursive process, which is thought. As the meaner—an aware selfhood—produces meaning from the signs engaged during the walk, the meaner produces a new self. Reflection, or higher order consciousness, unlike the remembered present, primary consciousness, seems based in the capacity to use signs, which is to say, the meaner must recognize not only the thing perceived but something else as well. The dog may recognize the rolled up newspaper as a potential threat to its safety, but I do not believe that it is capable of removing the flattened newspaper (or magazine) from its place on the floor to prevent its potential use. Since the learning to which I refer involves a categorization based on a background of value that results in adaptive change in behavior, then the ability to learn derives from activities that stem from value and the ability to use symbolic systems and that lead to adaptive change in behavior. These changes are a product not only of primary consciousness—of having images in the present—that continues to exist and interact with the mechanism of higher order consciousness, but of the building of a self through affective intersubjective exchanges. Using the lexicon of the world of signs, of which language is a significant sign-system, "the conceptual centers of the brain treat the symbols and their references and the imagery they evoke as an 'independent' world to be further categorized" (Edelman 1992, 150). In other words, that other perception of the evocation of the image is situated in a past and points toward a future; that perception is evidence of a self. This characteristic of secondary, or higher order consciousness, this ability to "construct a socially based selfhood, to model the world in terms of the past and the future, and to be directly aware" (Edelman 1992, 125), depends on symbolic memory of which language and art are of primary importance.

Now symbolic memory may arise naturally—indeed, language learning is apparently a natural process.[13] But development of symbolic memory requires an engagement with the world, even if, as Emily Dickinson might suggest, one does not actually venture far into it. Like Henry David Thoreau, Emily Dickinson traveled great distances without ever leaving her home. It was her investment in symbolic systems—language—that freed her from the confines of the immediate present and facilitated her ability to redesign herself.

> Between the form of Life and Life
> The difference is as big
> As Liquor at the Lip between
> And Liquor in the Jug
> The latter—excellent to keep—
> But for ecstatic need
> The corkless is superior—
> I know for I have tried (487)

Dickinson seems to know that she must venture out if she is to learn. She must take chances.

> So I must baffle at the Hint
> And cipher at the Sign
> And make much blunder, if at last
> I take the clue divine—

---

[13] I do not mean that language per se would arise in the absence of social interaction. Rather, I mean that without being taught, language is learned by all children without effort.

Emily Dickinson engaged language and the poetic form to break the confines of the immediate; and during her journey she maintained her contact with the world in her symbolic production. Her choice was to send letters:[14] postcards had not yet been invented.[15]

It is this capacity for self-awareness that explains the dramatic change in the walker such that return to home is made impossible. This walk that Thoreau describes so vividly is an intimate engagement with the world in which engagement the participant changes commensurate with the transformation of the world in which the traveler walks. Robert Frost has suggested something similar in the now cliched and more sinister poem "The Road Less Traveled." There, too, return is prevented and determining ("I took the road less traveled and that has made all the difference"), though the fortuitousness of Frost's decision has always made me very uneasy, especially since this poem has been read at so many high school graduation ceremonies. Thoreau, on the other hand, suggests that the walk not only is undertaken willfully but is an endeavor in which return is never a consideration; the Thoravian walk is a conscious leaving home—even one to which one might in body return after the walk. The consciousness that results, however, is founded in the body that walks. In the walking becomes the walker.

Stuck Inside of Mobile with the Memphis Blues Again

I think that to take a walk is to engage in curriculum. And I think that the efficacy of this walk depends on the ability of the walker to employ and extend symbolic memory in its several forms. Schools and curriculum are one place where that development might take place. I have dealt elsewhere (Block 1995) with the effects of contemporary practices of language learning—language arts instruction—on children's capacity to think freely. Although we talk liberally of the necessity for criti-

---

[14] This is my letter to the World
  That never wrote to Me . . .
[15] For a theoretical and curricular exploration of postcards see Block and Klein (1996).

cal thinking, we design our educational systems to prevent such practice. Schools are designed to promote reflection or self-awareness. Schools are organized to "produce good citizens," a phrase that usually means good workers. Indeed, all of our instruction is organized to prevent journeying or walking. First, seat time in the majority of schools is the means by which credits may be awarded. Carnegie units still dominate the curricular scene. From that stationary seat, walking in the sense we have defined it here is not possible. There is no interaction with an environment; indeed, as William Pinar (1975) bitterly notes, the anatomically irregular furniture of the schools teaches students to ignore the discomfort of their bodies.

Second, curriculum is organized to keep children on track, on task, and on time. Fully observable, children in school are not permitted the freedom of the Thoravian walk; indeed, schools are organized to prevent the experience of adventure or lostness. Children not in step with other children are classified quickly, remediated, and/or drugged. National curricula and/or standards should further determine the paths along which children might journey.

Third, the disconnectedness of curriculum precludes the ability of the student to follow an idea—to reflect. Linearity governs the organization of experiences and learning and restricts possibility of thought. Following an idea to create a path is impossible when school days are carefully segmented into subject periods.

Fourth, schools by their nature are today disconnected from the society in which they function. As Howard Gardner notes (1991, 138), "Schools are institutions that place together individuals who have not known one another, to work on tasks that appear more or less remote from the operations of the remainder of society." Lostness in school is a product of isolation that is systemic; finding oneself requires removal from the system.

Finally, schools address a social image of the learner and thus aim at a target that does not exist. What Gardner calls "the unschooled mind"[16] of the five-year-old—the mind of the

---

[16] Remember that by mind I refer to that which arises out of the brain and for which the body supplies content.

child that has learned the world informally during the daily un-school life, the mind that learns language and makes hypotheses about the myriad objects in the world—remains in the school-age child and adult; unless this mind is addressed, formal schooling is irrelevant. Given what Gardner (1991, 78) refers to as streams of development that engage various modes of symbolization (event or role structuring in language systems, topological mapping, digital mapping and notation), learning must be organized to highlight these waves of symbolization. Clearly, this is best accomplished not only in activity that engages these waves but also in activities in which symbol making is intrinsically interesting to the learner. Learning, or conceptual categorization based upon value, as I have suggested, depends on *qualia*. That which in the present cannot be connected to the past by a constructed self to anticipate a future may be potentially influential but may be so only unconsciously.

Thoreau (1961, 410) tells us that "The child should have the advantage of ignorance as well as of knowledge, and is fortunate if he gets his share of neglect and exposure." It is our intent that our society be an educated one. I have attempted in this chapter to suggest that to effect this end we give up our will to control and offer the child opportunity for exposure. The capacity for lostness is the beginning of educative experience. The experience of schooling today is organized to develop mind and body as if they were two separate entities. Physical education is a separate class in most curricula. What I have suggested in this chapter is that the separation of the physical from the mental denies the reality of mind and promotes an education that denies learning. And then we blame our children for the world we made. It's alright, ma, I'm only bleeding.

Chapter VII

School as the Product of the Adult Fantasy of a World Without Children

. . . the education of children is an extremely useful index to the values of the society of adults.

Michael Zuckerman

The School and the Pied Piper of Hamelin

It is a warm day in late summer: August 26, 1994, to be exact. It is Monday morning about 9:00 a.m., and as has been my wont I am running in the streets. I run roughly six miles a day— fifty minutes or so—on each of the weekday mornings. In a sense I consider this exercise an engagement with the community through which I run. Today, however, I notice that it is exceptionally and unusually quiet out here in the streets. Quiet and empty except for my cadenced step and rhythmic breathing. There is something amiss about this community this morning. For the past several months we have experienced summer vacation, and I am accustomed to the scream of children at play, the sight of children about the streets, the sharing of the roads with children riding bicycles heading somewhere and nowhere. Today, however, I feel strange and estranged; these are not the streets to which I have been accustomed. There is no one about. The streets are barren. I am veritably alone. Friday, I recall, it had been different out here.

Today is actually the first day of school in Wisconsin. Unlike in New York where I grew up and where I worked in the public schools for seventeen years and where school traditionally begins the Tuesday after Labor Day, in this midwestern state the school year begins in the final weeks of August. I suspect that rooted in rural cultures the school calendar in Wisconsin, as in other farming communities in the Midwest, remains more firmly tied to the planting and harvest schedules than it does in urban areas, and especially in the New York City schools. I recall that regular school attendance in a culture predominantly rural was historically based on the conditions of the fields and the physical ability to work in them: school sessions were usually confined to six to eight weeks and occurred when children as workers—and mostly older children at that—were deemed unnecessary at home. During the first decade of the nineteenth century, the residents of Franklin, Massachusetts, for example, raised about one hundred dollars to pay a teacher to keep the winter school for six or seven weeks "for the older children whose labor was needed less on the farm during this season" (Messerli 1972, 12). The younger children would be sent to school much more regularly and during several seasons because they were not capable of helping with the planting or the harvest. They needed as well to be kept out of the way. During the winter months, men would usually assume the role of teacher because during these colder months the bigger boys would be in attendance and women were assumed incapable of handling them.

Schools have always been required to adjust their schedules and personnel to the exigencies and demands of the outside world; sessions were usually timed around the needs of the fields and the adult Christian calendar: winter break occurred at Christmas time and spring break occurred about Easter; summers as vacation from school existed because of the need for workers during the planting and harvest schedules. In New England a week for skiing closed the schools where attendance was probably sparse anyway due to the amount of fallen snow: it became convenient to declare a skiing holiday. Here in Wisconsin school is frequently closed the week or two prior to Thanksgiving to permit the children to engage in the rites of the fall hunting season. Here in the North it is good to be inside during the winter months; it is appropriate, which is to say convenient, to have school during these shortening days and colder temperatures.

I am a professor of education at the university. And as I run past the school, these thoughts disturb my mind. When I run I usually anticipate enclosure in a very private world of thought, and often when I am running successfully the outside world, in gestalist terms, becomes the background for the figures of my thought. As I run through the environment, I may be conscious of it as I might be when I drive: focused somewhere else but aware of where I am because I expect it to be there. I may be safely lost. But today as I run, I am uncomfortable and troubled, unsettled but not lost. I remain particularly focused on the background, on the environment: the streets are unusually silent and empty and that red brick building past which I run seems so solidly positioned. That edifice, too, like these streets through which I run seems inordinately silent. As I run past the one-story brick building where I have this morning left my daughter, I am suddenly aware that the unquiet silence of the streets is the result of the occupation by the school of the children of our community. All of our children are in school. They are, as it were, captured.

I think of the story of the Pied Piper of Hamelin. You will recall that in this perhaps apocryphal tale the Piper had contracted to rid the town of Hamelin of a plague of rats. Playing upon his pipe he lured the rats out of town, and by various accounts either led them by his fluting to their deaths in the river or just plain away from the town. Alarmed that they had promised so much money for the Piper's services and appalled that the mere sounds of the flute had accomplished what they had in all of their endeavors been incapable of achieving and cognizant that the rats were, indeed, now gone forever, the mayor of the town with the support, I suppose, of his citizenry refused the Piper his wages. Haughtily dismissing the unpaid servant, the townsfolk returned to their daily lives self-satisfied and free of the pesky vermin. The rats were gone, the Piper brushed off. But the children remained.

Soon, however, the Piper reappeared. The tale continues (Lemieux 1987, n.p):

> Then one morning the townspeople heard the soft tones of a pipe, and they realized the Piper had returned. As he played his strange and wonderful music, all the children of Hamelin gathered around him, singing, laughing and dancing.

The Piper had returned for his pay: it was the children he now sought for his wages and as he played his flute they followed his music out of the town. In his version of the tale, Robert Browning (1973) writes that:

> The Mayor was dumb, and the Council stood
> As if they were changed into blocks of wood,
> Unable to move a step, or cry
> To the children merrily skipping by—
> And could only follow with the eye
> that joyous crowd at the Piper's back . . .
> When lo, as they reached the mountain's side,
> A wonderous portal opened wide,
> As if a cave was suddenly hollowed;
> And the Piper advanced and the children followed,
> And when all were in to the very last,
> The door in the mountain-side shut fast.

The children having been entranced by the strains of the Piper and following his melodies are led away by him to be . . . well, some say captured and others seduced, but in any case lost to the town forever.[1] I cannot help thinking of another story in which the rock was rolled not *before* but *away* from a cave's entrance, but that is, as I say, another tale; the story of the Resurrection and the promise of hope upon which it is based stands in marked contrast to the story of the Pied Piper and the loss of the children. In "The Pied Piper of Hamelin" the children disappear forever and are forever lost to the world. If ever they appear on earth again it is not as children but as fully grown adults. Browning writes:

> And I must not omit to say
> That in Transylvania there's a tribe
> Of alien people that ascribe
> The outlandish ways and dress
> On which their neighbours lay such stress,
> To their fathers and mothers having risen
> Out of some subterraneous prison
> Into which they were trepanned
> Long time ago in a mighty band
> Out of Hamelin town in Brunswick land,
> But how or why they don't understand.

---

[1] In one version of the tale a lame child is excluded from the community of children because he cannot keep pace with his companions and the stone rolls before the cave entrance before he can enter. Perhaps special educators reflect upon the interpretation of this aspect of the tale.

There is no resurrection in this tale; rather, I sense here an ultimate loss. And what is lost it would seem are the children! This tale of the Pied Piper is a strange and familiar one to me. It is the story at least of the literal loss of children. Ostensibly it is a morality tale told to adults to remind them that their greatest asset is not their money but their progeny. They should not be so greedy or they may lose their children.[2] But the choice of metaphor and structure concerns me. Rats and children: what is the equation? Why would the tellers of this tale make both rats and children susceptible to the piper's strains. The piper (who is he?) makes both disappear, the former to their obvious death and the latter to . . . well, where can we say they go except away from the adults. I consider what equates the two elements seduced by the piper's strains. Both the vermin and the children are constantly underfoot, create a mess and consume a huge quantity of food. They are both in the end bothersome and costly! In this overdetermined tale the strains of the piper lure the children out of the town and there is nothing the citizenry can do to hold the children back. Was there no music like this in the town before? Were the children simply entranced as had been the rats? Admittedly we must teach our children to be wary of strangers, but would none of the children heed their parents' warnings?

I think that no one could invent such a tale but people for whom children were expendable. Who could imagine the loss of a whole population of children except people who unconsciously wished it? What did the tellers imagine would be lost in the loss of children and what might have been gained by their disappearance? I wonder what could have been transpiring in the minds of the children as they were piped to the cave where they were held captive. Versions of the legend suggest that they were taken to a land where "waters gushed and fruit-trees grew,/And flowers put forth a fairer hue,/ And everything was strange and new . . ." I think about the children and I wonder, did they know they were prisoners held for ransom? I ask again, were they following the strains of music so rarely

---

[2] Benjamin Braddock in the film *The Graduate* spurns his parents' values as well, but Braddock is a college graduate in his early twenties. The tale of the Pied Piper speaks of young children probably all under the age of thirteen; materialistic values are of little concern to them.

heard in the hard town? Were the children entranced by the stranger who in his melodies promised them fun and excitement that was not part of their daily existence in the town? Is this, then, the text of the tale: the children demanded more of the town than the townspeople were prepared to offer, and for the physical and psychological peace of the town the children had to be, as it were, disappeared. Once ensconced within the cave, I wonder, what did the children think had happened? How did they make sense of their experience? What did they do within the cave once they were held captive there? Did they learn anything in the cave? Who were they when they finally exited the cave as adults? In Browning's tale they are at best eccentric, but what could that mean?

I think about the origins of the story of the Pied Piper of Hamelin. They are certainly not with the children. Indeed, I find the roots of this story steeped in a dislike of childhood and a wish for its disappearance. I think the Pied Piper is a story of children lost as a product of the selfish concerns of the adult world. The story for all its nostalgia does not seem to like children very much. The same strains that rid the town of vermin entranced the children to a similar fate. Both are eliminated from the town by the piper's music. Entrapped within the cave they were no longer children in this world; adult concern for children was no longer necessary. When these children exited from the cave, they did so as adults; they were no longer children in this world. Finally, the Pied Piper seems to me to be about a world rid of children. The noise and clutter of the streets are eliminated with the loss of both the rats and the children. The townspeople, selling their children for pieces of gold and silver (I think here of the story of Joseph and his brothers and of Jesus' betrayal by Judas Iscariot), are left with a world unencumbered with the concerns of children and their childhoods. Ah yes, they miss their children, but the quiet is so extraordinary and uncommon.

So I think of the story of the Pied Piper as I run. And I think of the story's relation to school. You see, I begin to think that school is the vast cave to which the children today have been piped; that solid red brick building over there is the cave to which our laughing and dancing children have been led. I am alarmed as I suddenly realize that *school may be the product of an adult fantasy of a world without children!* And I alarmingly consider that I have left my child there this morning!! Needless to say, though I will say it anyway, ensconced within the school-cave sits my daughter and the sons and daughters of the other townspeople. I wonder, with whom did we negotiate in such bad faith to have lost our children to this place, and at what cost may I retrieve our daughters and sons if it is yet possible. I, for one, missed the piper's strains.

In this chapter I would like to look at the construction of the school as the product of the adult fantasy of a world without children. I do not intend this to be an exhaustive history of education in the world generally nor in the United States specifically, but I would like to examine some of the educational discourses of the American experience and to look at them in light of the discourses of the folktale of the Pied Piper of Hamelin. To understand the invention of the school in America as the creation of adults who would be rid of their children may offer some insight into the problems we now face in education and suggest some directions education might pursue for the future, both its own future and that of our children. Nor do I mean to essentialize the educational experiences of the American populace. I am aware that the experiences of children in school differ according to race, gender, social class, and region of the country (see for example, Nasaw 1979; Katz 1973; Gutek 1991; Perkinson 1991). But I would like to suggest that what links these school experiences is the idea of the school as a holding tank for children and of a world freed by the absence of children for the activity of adults.

Education and the Values of Adult Society

Michael Zuckerman (1973, 28) writes that the values that adult society wishes to deliver "must be transmitted in terms so simple that even a child can understand them." The school has always been the instrument of that adult society desiring to transform children into adults in the neatest and most efficient ways. The schools have also been employed by the adult society to keep the children separate from it in both a psychological and a physical sense. That is, schools have been organized to protect the society of the adult from that of the child and vice versa; in either case, the world was made free if not of children then certainly of childhood. In this mission, schools have been inordinately successful. Zuckerman (1973, 28) notes that "Children who grew up in provincial Massachusetts grew up in a society that insisted on concord and consensus; as they grew they became, subtly, almost irresistibly, people who could live in such a society." Similarly, Perkinson (1991, 3) writes that some strong cultural origins of school exist in the exigencies of adult life: "Forced to spend their days securing the basic necessities of life, these pioneer parents had little time to care for their children." Schools were the perfect repository for their offspring. David Nasaw (1979, 11) writes that poor children throughout the 1820s were regularly removed from their natural parents "to be placed in newly established institutions: asylums, reform schools, and orphanages, where they would be isolated from their parents and placed under twenty-four-hour institutional control."[3] George Dennison (1969, 80) writes of the educational experience of Jose: "One could not say he had been schooled at all, but rather for five years he had been indoctrinated in the contempt of persons, for contempt of persons had been the supreme fact demonstrated in the classrooms, and referred alike to teachers, parents, and children. For all practical purposes, Jose's inability to learn consisted precisely of his school-induced behavior." And Diane Ravitch (1995, 374) declares that "no school is truly successful unless it provides students with the opportunity to learn challenging subject matter." What she refers to is the setting of high standards in mathematics and science, in history, English, geography, the arts, and foreign languages.

> When adopted by a state, these curriculum frameworks—describing what every child in the state should know and be able to do in each subject—should become the basis for realigning assessments, teacher education, and textbooks to high standards. Once a state (or a community, or a school) decides what it wants children to learn, then it should take steps to ensure that teachers master what they are supposed to teach, and that the tests used are reliable indicators of the extent to which children are actually achieving high standards.

---

[3] I think of the recent proposals of the Republican majority for the reintroduction of orphanages as a cure for social ills.

The child, then, is conceptualized as the empty vessel into which the state might pour its standardized materials and who ought to be administered by the state's hired vassals. The school is conceptualized as the cave into which children are piped and where they might be maintained until they are suitable for adult society. What might be considered challenging to the child has been established by the society from which that child arrives into the school and into which s/he must subsequently return; those standards have little to do with the child but rather what that child must become. Immersed in this curriculum, the child has been, as it were, enticed into the cave to exit finally as either the conforming adult or the miscreant social outcast. Larry Cuban, in his book *How Teachers Taught* (1993, 249-50) writes that

> The overriding purpose of the school, not always explicit but nonetheless evident, is to inculcate into children the prevailing social norms, values, and behaviors that will prepare them for economic, social, and political participation in the larger culture. How schools are organized . . . what knowledge is highly valued . . . administrator and teacher beliefs and attitudes toward cultural differences, and certain pedagogical practices . . . mirror the norms, beliefs, and practices of the larger socioeconomic system.

Schools are where we pipe our children until they are deemed ready for our society. Out here is no place to be a child.

Of course, these practices are premised on foundational beliefs in the identities of childhood and society, but it is nonetheless obvious that schools are conceptualized as a place to safely keep the children from society and, likewise, as a locus to supervise children in order to safely maintain adult society. Ironically, in language that recalls to me the tale of the Pied Piper, William Torrey Harris, that giant of educational history, once described education as the process "by which the individual is elevated into the species." Thus, exiting from the cave into which they had been consigned by adults, the children return to the world as adults having been trained to be such by the materials of the curriculum. The disappearance of childhood decried by critics such as Neil Postman (1994) seems to me a misnomer; childhood rather than disappearing has simply been banished to the school where it is condemned to eradication. Schools are organized to secure the child and eliminate childhood. Although the school acknowledges the child, it refuses it childhood. Decrying what he describes as the disappearance of childhood during the modern period, Postman (1994, 151) declares that school "is the only public institution left to us based on the assumption that there are important differences between childhood and adulthood and that adults have things of value to teach children." I am not consoled. I am more in sympathy with Herman Melville who writes at the death of Bartleby, the Scrivener, "Ah Bartleby, ah humanity." It's alright, ma, I'm only bleeding.

It is of course, impossible to talk of the school without also discussing childhood. I will, however, save a more complete discussion of this for a later chapter and attempt here to merely note how schools derived from the desire to control what would come to be called children. Indeed, the development of schools has been linked to the invention of childhood (see Ariès 1965; Block 1995) and to the adult insistence that the child itself be contained and rehearsed within the enclosure of the school, to ensure upon exit the presence of an adult who it is hoped will be satisfactory to the grown-up world. Even Postman (1994, 46) writes "The capacity to control and overcome one's nature became one of the defining characteristics of adulthood and therefore one of the essential purposes of education; for some, *the* essential purpose of education." Schools have always existed in the sense that specialized arenas were established and/or accepted for the training of young citizens,[4] but it is also clear to me that the formal establishment of schools during the medieval period was a product of the desire to hold within the confines of that school people (who would come to be known as children) who required education—or protection—in order to be adults. Schools as we know them developed parallel to the adult conception of the child and the perceived needs of the students who were to occupy those schools. In America, schools served the dual purpose of protecting children from a

---

[4] What I mean here is that early Greek schools, for example, were established for the children of the elite. Chiron, the first teacher, was the teacher of the children of the gods. "Only a small minority of the Greek population of the Alexandrian world were ever able to take full advantage of [the school]" (Reimer 1971, 76). Indeed, the elite, which is to say the wealthy, have always had first access to education.

corrupt world and protecting that world from unredeemed children. Education was a means of separating the world from its children.

Early American ideas concerning education were not child-centered though they were concerned with children. As Michael Katz (1987) notes, during these early years of the American colonial period there were not systems of education but rather an establishment of schools for the education of the young. The purpose of the school was to protect children from themselves and to direct them away from childhood freedoms and toward adult beliefs and practices. The old deluder satan law required that townships containing fifty householders "shall forthwith appoint one within their towne to teach all such children as shall resort to him to write & reade." The purpose of this education was to ensure that men be made familiar with the scriptures "so that the true sence and meaning of the original might not be clouded by false glosses of saint seeming deceivers." Towns of one hundred families were required to establish grammar schools so " . . . that the more thereof [are] able to instruct youth so far as they shall be fitted for the university." Church leaders were trained at these universities. As I have discussed elsewhere (Block 1995) this pedagogy of reading was premised on the idea that truths of texts were inherent in them and that reading was the practice of getting that meaning. Reading was the pedagogy of getting the right meaning, a product that was already known at the outset by the civil and religious authorities; a whole pedagogy of reading was established by this hermeneutic. This reading pedagogy became the basis for curriculum and was established to ensure the moral rigor of the Puritan purpose. Its function was to deny the child in order to advocate for the world of the adult; it was to ensure the soul of the child by confining it in a disciplined ideology whose purpose was to educate the child to be an adult. Two hundred years later Horace Mann (1969, 50) would argue that the purposes of education "are to preserve the good and to repudiate the evil which now exist, and give scope to the sublime law of progression." That good to which Mann clung inhered in the values of the (white, male, middle class, Christian) adult community and which he meant to perpetuate in the educational systems he advocated establishing.

Later, with the changing conceptions of childhood and the invention of adolescence, schools became specialized structures for containing those children until they were ready for the adult world, that is, until they were adults. "We are changed and become good," Robert Cleaver and John Dod wrote in 1621, "not by birth but by education" (in Postman 1994, 47). Conversely, these schools kept these children out of the adult world protecting *it* from *them*.[5] The function of education was (as it is now) the indoctrination of the child into adult ways of thought and the separation of the child from the adult world.

No doubt the early citizens believed (variously) that such education was necessary for the salvation of the child's soul; nevertheless, the uneducated child represented a threat to the human community merely because they were children. "A wise son maketh a glad father, but a foolish son is the grief of his mother" is the alphabet lesson for youth for the letter "A",[6] and for the letter "F" the child would read, "Foolishness is bound up in the heart of a child, but the rod of correction will drive it far from him." Childhood was a condition best eliminated. Clearly, during these early years of the nation, the home was largely responsible for the education of the young, the place where they could be indoctrinated about the world and how they were to behave in it. The development of formal schools, however irregular and as informal as sessions in them might be, might be understood as *systems* to remove children from the temptations of the world where they were susceptible; to remove them from the adult world where they might, unredeemed as they were, tempt adults even as they might be tempted by them.

Schools were also institutions that would keep irritating children away from the adults. On the one hand, children might be redeemed by the adult attentions of which education was only a single form. From a later period I recall Hawthorne's *The Scarlet Letter* (1959, 93), which speaks of the control of chil-

---

[5] I am reminded of the question asked the Rabbi of Anatevka in *Fiddler on the Roof*: "Rabbi," one of the townspeople asks, "is there a prayer for the Czar?" "Yes," the Rabbi responds, "May God bless and keep the Czar—far away from us."

[6] As was of course, "In Adam's fall we sinn'd all."

dren: "The discipline of the family, in those days, was of a far more rigid kind than now. The frown, the harsh rebuke, the frequent application of the rod, enjoined by Scriptural authority, were used, not merely in the way of punishment for actual offences, but as a wholesome regimen." Children were to be indoctrinated into adult beliefs for the sakes of their souls—and those of the adults. On the other hand, the world had to be protected from the corrupt souls of children. The horror of the Salem witch trials of 1692, I believe, may be understood partially as a fear of children. That is, of sixty-seven persons accused of being possessed in New England between 1620 and 1725 over half, thirty-six, were under the age of twenty (Karlsen 1987, 224). Whether the behavior of these children was conceived as such an aberration to the community that they had to be possessed or whether these children were so terrified of their own inclinations that they believed themselves possessed, the fact remains that an enormous percentage of the accused were of what we would know as school-age children. Michael Zuckerman (1973, 29) writes: "The premise of Puritan education was precisely this conviction of corruption [in the child] and the consequent necessity to pour in good things from without." As the populace grew and became less manageable, the schools assumed the role of indoctrinating the children.

Schools seem always to have been instruments of such control. Clearly our Puritan ancestors utilized schools such as they were to contain the potentially disastrous inclinations of youth. Joseph Illick (1974, 328) in his essay "Anglo-American Child-Rearing" notes that "Breaking the will of the child was based on the supposition that the parents' will could be substituted. The child would doubt his own abilities, repress his strivings and look to a higher authority." Diane Ravitch's advocacy for higher standards quoted above is a contemporary version of this process. Schools were also, John Walzer (1974) states, one way to be rid of children without having to send them off to relatives. Schools, particularly in those rural settings, could be understood as loci of both abandonment and retention. Parents could be rid of their children over the course of the day and yet be assured that those same children were being indoctrinated into the values held by their parents. It is this argument that still bestirs adult communities concerning curriculum issues—hence the battles over multiculturalism and the rainbow curriculum and the perennial spate of banning books.

Schools were the cave into which children were confined until they could be useful to themselves or could be called adults. Schools "were an important part of inculcating proper attitudes and ideals, and at the same time a place of confinement and protection . . . What children in school were protected from was a world which offered too much freedom" (Walzer 1974, 368). Although the educational ideals of Benjamin Franklin, Thomas Jefferson, and Noah Webster loom large in educational history, each of these three proposed an education calling "for a new kind of civic education that was suited to the economic, social and political needs of the new republic" (Gutek, 1991). Children would be educated to take their places in a republican society. Horace Mann (1969, 16) would write that

> the consequences of a virtuous education, at the end of twenty-one years, are now precisely the same as they would be, if, at the end of twenty-one days after his birth, the infant had risen from his cradle into the majestic form of manhood, and were possessed of all those qualities and attributes, which a being created in the image of God *ought to have*;—with a power of fifty years of beneficent labor; labor compacted into his frame; with nerves of sympathy, reaching out from his own heart and twining around the heart of society, so that the great social wants of men should be a part of consciousness;—and with a mind able to perceive what is right, promptly to defend it, or if need be, to die for it.

To Horace Mann education could actually occur in a vacuum, a veritable cave. The virtuous education of which he speaks would produce a wonderful being despite every other aspect of the world. Mann posits the school as a enclosure wherein children might be protected from the world so that they might enter into that world upon exiting the school—cave as able citizens prepared, even, as we have since learned, to die for that world.[7] Needless to say, this society was based on patrician and/

---

[7] One theory explaining the derivation of the story of the Pied Piper concerns the marching off of the children to war in what has come to be known as The Children's Crusade.

or middle-class values and was decidedly white and male. Needless to say as well, Mann's conceptualization of the child reveals a change in fundamental beliefs of its character. Perhaps no longer originally damned, children might be understood now as blank slates on which society may be writ large—hence, for Mann, the necessity of good schooling and the proper training of teachers.

Joseph Kett (1974) notes that an important feature of early nineteenth century society was the subordination of young people and that this subordination, though secured to the tradition of the child as an inferior member of the family, became an attitude less bound to land ownership and acquisition than had previously existed; thus, a social space was created into which young people might be slotted, and schools were a chief instrument in that creation. Whereas once the family organized the social development of the child by assigning land to the eldest male child, now schools could assume that role. Where once parents could order the lives of their children, schools were now the means of that control. In 1809 William Beaumont would write his brother that "Errors and improprieties will beset you on every side in spite of your precautionary efforts to evade them. The strongest and most effectual barrier against these deviations is to cultivate your mind and procure a stock of familiar ideas and useful information" (in Kett 1974, 46). The advice of family would be taken up and proffered by the schools. Schools, it could be argued, could become caretakers and nurturers of the children and could do so by putting youth in their place and by placing before them stocks of familiar ideas and useful information.

As primogeniture declined in influence in society, and as American society became more secular, schools assumed the role of keeping children in their places: of denying children the play of children. Kett (1974, 47) writes that although "public shaming [the stocks] was no longer a primary method for maintaining social order among adults, [it] continued to flourish in the schools." Emerson would write that "Something must be done [about the schools]. . . . In their distress the wisest are tempted to adopt violent means, to proclaim martial law, corporal punishment, mechanical arrangements, bribes, spies, wrath, main strength and ignorance, in place of that wise and genial providential influence they had hoped, and yet hope in some future day to adopt." The world that was so organized controlled the appearances of children in it and severely controlled their behaviors in it. Schools played a key role here: Ralph Waldo Emerson (1982, 221) writes in 1839 that "We are shut up in schools & college recitation rooms for ten or fifteen years & come out at last with a bellyful of words & do not know a thing . . . The farm is a piece of the world, the School house is not." His later caution in 1856 offers some indication not only of the contemporary life in schools but of their ideological foundations as well; school clearly did not offer to children what he proposed should be paramount in the lives of children. Rather, Emerson understood that schools were no place for the child (Emerson 1982, 467):

> Don't let them eat seed-corn; don't let them anticipate, or ante-date, & be young men, before they have finished their boyhood. Let them have the fields & woods, & learn their secret & the base & foot-ball, & wrestling, & brickbats, & suck all the strength & courage that lies for them in these games; let them ride bareback, & catch their horse in his pasture, let them hood & spear their fish, & shin a post and a tall tree, & shoot their partridge & trap the woodchuck, before they begin to dress like collegians, & sing in serenades, & make polite calls.

Emerson recognized that children must play lest their minds become morbidly diseased, but schools were understood as essential for keeping children out of the world and controlling their play. "Keep them within doors at their book, at some little service," the minister John Barnard (Walzer 1974, 373) warns his congregation, speaking of the children. And though it was acknowledged that children must have time in which to play, the ambivalence felt about children during the eighteenth century had influence on the development of schools in the United States.

It is not necessary to emphasize too much that schools could be conceptualized as holding environments and that their primary function was the control of children; this function of the school not only permitted but often required the exercise of physical coercion and punishment. It is important to note that what appears to be abusive behavior toward children in the schools was an extension of the idea that schools were where children were to be kept until they became adults; monies for education forever are parsimoniously offered. Horace Mann

(1969, 24), arguing for larger school building appropriations, notes that "a healthful, comfortable schoolhouse can be erected as cheaply as one, which, judging from its construction, you would say, had been dedicated to the evil genius of deformity and suffering." Mann sarcastically notes that schoolrooms offer excellent lessons in geography because a child could move a mere five rows and traverse through several climatic states. It is clear that the school building represented adult values regarding education as well as the adult desire to keep the children ensconced within the structure. No wonder truancy becomes a problem.

Furthermore, teachers were often ill equipped to practice their profession, and the pay was barely at a subsistence level. Nonetheless, the teacher's authority was considered absolute though in reality the availability of teachers called that authority into doubt. The primary purpose of the school seems to have been control of the children, and all means and techniques were acceptable. Educational psychology merely offers less violent means of control, and theories of motivation assume a lack of intrinsic interest in the material. Too often, however, resort to physical punishment was a means of control. The school itself as a penal colony is best exemplified by such treatment of students; Horace Mann (1969, 23) wrote in 1837 that

> I have seen schoolhouses, in central districts of rich and populous towns, where each seat connected with a desk, consisted only of an upright post or pedestal, jutting up out of the floor, the upper end of which was only abut eight or ten inches square, without side-arms or backboard; and some of them so high that the feet of the children in vain sought after the floor. They were beyond soundings. Yet on the top of these stumps, the masters and misses of the school must balance themselves, as they can, for six hours in a day. All attempts to preserve silence in such a house are not only vain, but cruel. Nothing but absolute impalement could keep a live child still, on such a seat; and you would hardly think him worth living, if it could.

Of course it could not be that children would sit quietly for this amount of time and so teachers would resort to physical punishment to further their authority. Corporal punishment was not only permitted but even encouraged. Schoolmaster Felton, having beaten a child's hand until his hand turned black and being threatened with civic action by the child's father, was assured by Colonel Barnes that "the law was very favorable to schoolmasters" (Walzer 1974, 369). Even when more enlightened teachers abandoned actual corporal punishment (perhaps for fear of retribution after school by the child's husky out-of-school friends) they resorted to other forms of cruel and unusual punishment. Mann (1969, 45) notes sarcastically that

> To imprison timid children in a dark and solitary place; to brace open the jaws with a piece of wood; to torture the muscles and bones, by the strain of an unnatural position, or of holding an enormous weight; to inflict a wound upon the instinctive feelings of modesty and delicacy, by making a girl sit with the boys or go out with them at recess; to bring a whole class around a fellow-pupil, to ridicule and shame him; to break the spirit of self-respect, by enforcing some ignominious compliance; to give a nick-name—these and such as these, are the gentle appliances by which some teachers, who profess to discard corporal punishment, maintain the empire of the schoolroom;—as though muscles and bones were less corporeal than the skin; as though a wound of the spirit were of less moment than one of the flesh; and the body's blood more sacred than the soul's purity.

Mann never denies the efficacy of corporal punishment, but rather criticizes its vicious and indiscriminate use. Finally the purpose of such punishment is to ensure conformity and assist control. Mann (1969, 318) admonishes that "It is better, therefore, to tolerate punishment, in cases where the teacher has no other resource, than to suffer insubordination or disobedience in our schools." Schools were where children were sent to protect them from the adult world, but at the same time we might say that schools preserved the world from children. At the same time, schools were meant to turn children into adults. The ostensible purpose of school was the education of children, but in fact, both the subject matters and the manners were meant to deny the reality of childhood.

The development of schools during the nineteenth and twentieth centuries also suggests them to be products of the adult fantasy of a world without children. On the one hand, we may look to the feminization of teaching as a means of understanding this construction of the school. In this view schools were organized as alternative families to which children would be sent to be away from their reputedly ineffective and often immoral (by developing middle-class standards) natural families. Madeleine Grumet (1988, 39) notes that "The common school movement and the feminization of teaching colluded in support of a program of centralized education that exploited the status and integrity of the family to strip it of its authority and deliver its children to the state." Organized predominantly by men and aided by the industrialization of the United States where men were employable out of the home for wages they could not earn within it, schools were staffed by women whose care of the young, Mann (1969, 26) would note, "is one of the clearest ordinances of nature [that] woman is the appointed guide and guardian of children of a tender age." Needless to say, it is not the mother but the female teacher who is appointed as guide and guardian, it being acknowledged that the family no longer could be depended upon to educate the child in ways the ruling powers believed necessary for the continuation of the society to which they were becoming accustomed. David Nasaw (1979, 77) quotes the Boston School Committee dictum of 1853:

> The parent is not the absolute owner of the child. The child is a member of a community, has certain rights, and is bound to perform certain duties, and so far as these relate to the public, government has the same right to control over the child, that it has over the parent. . . Those children should be brought within the jurisdiction of the Public Schools, from whom, through their vagrant habits, our property is most in danger and so, of all others, most need the protecting power of the State.

The traditional role of the family in the education of the child was given to the schools presided over now not by the mother but by her surrogate who would be taught to treat other people's children as she would never treat her own.[8] Children were sent to school to be made into adults who might benefit the State; until that time the children were safely entombed within the school's walls.

Michael Katz (1987) has recounted how the schools in the nineteenth century became organized by the bureaucratic model under the influence of the power of the growing industrial hegemony of the country. Other models for organizing the schools were discarded, though rarely did an understanding of the child figure in the decision to adopt one model over

---

[8] See Madeleine Grumet, "Other People's Children" (1988).

another. The needs of adult society were always the criterion by which schools were to be constructed and organized. George Dennison (1969, 9), a voice in opposition to this trend, would find it necessary to say in the twentieth century, "The proper concern of a primary school is not education in a narrow sense, and still less preparation for larger life, but the present lives of the children." However, there is precious little in the language of education in the nineteenth century as the patterns of organization were being argued and formed that spoke of the lives of children. Rather, it was the lives to which children were to be trained that was the topic of discourse. "School," Everett Reimer (1971, 85) declares, "qualifies men [sic] for participation in other institutions and convicts those who do not meet the requirements of school of not deserving desirable roles in other institutions." The decision to adopt the bureaucratic model accorded with developing industrial modes of production and the fantastic growth of cities as a result of industrial growth and the concomitant exodus to the cities from rural environments. In 1845 the Boston School Committee would argue that its task was

> to take children at random from a great city, undisciplined, uninstructed, often with inveterate forwardness and obstinacy, and with the inherited stupidity of centuries of ignorant ancestors; forming them from animals into intellectual beings; and, so far as a school can do it, from intellectual beings into spiritual beings; giving to many their first appreciation of what is wise, what is true, what is lovely, and what is pure, and not merely their first impressions, but what may be their only impressions (in Katz, 1987, 48).

Schools in this model were conceptualized as the cave into which children might be piped that they might be transformed from rude and/or innocent savages[9] to civilized adults. Mann (1969, 175) wrote that "We should transfuse our best sentiments, transplant our best ideas and habits, into the receptive soul of childhood. It is our duty to separate the right from the wrong, in our own mind and conduct, and to incorporate the former only in the minds and conduct of children." Toward the end of the next century Dennison (1969, 9) would write,

---

[9] Linking children to Native Americans in the vocabulary also gives some indication of adult attitudes toward their offspring. Racial identity probably saved the lives of white children even as it massacred those of color.

"The present quagmire of public education is entirely the result of unworkable centralization and the lust for control that permeates every bureaucratic institution." We have piped our children into the schools where they are inextricably mired. It's alright, ma, I'm only bleeding.

At the beginning of the nineteenth century, Katz (1987) writes, several organizational possibilities for the development of public schooling vied for dominance. Of course each represented the desires of a specific interest group that founded educational concerns on a particular social vision. Education was premised on that vision even as it was meant to perpetuate it. Paternalistic voluntarism was one option offered for the organization of schooling and education. This paradigm found its advocates in well-to-do citizens who would contribute funds to the education of the children of the poor so as "to extend the means of education to such poor children as do not belong to, or are not provided for, by any religious society" (in Katz 25). That is, these children were to be educated in public institutions because their parents were considered incapable either financially or emotionally, or both, of providing education for them. It was the purpose of these institutions to remove children from their homes that they might be educated to take their part in adult society. Katz (1987, 27) writes that "Voluntarism was without question a class system of education. It provided a means for one class to civilize another and thereby ensure that society would remain tolerable, orderly, and safe." Of course, paternalistic voluntarism conceptualized schools as training grounds for future citizens and required that children be taken from their parents that they might be brought into society by those most capable of so initiating them. Katz (1987) quotes the New York Public School Society's attributing the low level of school attendance to "either . . . the extreme indigence of the parents . . . or their intemperance or vice; or . . . a blind indifference to the best interests of their offspring." Such "urchins instead of being useful members of the community, will become the burdens and pests of society." In this model the schools are easily conceptualized as the caves to which the children might be piped to rid the community of the depraved and needy.

Democratic localism was a strong alternative proposal to paternalistic voluntarism for the organizational structures of a school system. Democratic localism was based on the tradition of the local rural school, where the provincial district or community school was charged with the education of the children. Arguing that centralized schools denied the schooling that a community desired and required for their children, the advocates of this alternative argued that centralization, in the form say, of the Board of Education in Massachusetts (of which Horace Mann was the first secretary), "appeared to be the commencement of a system of centralization and of monopoly of power in a few hands, contrary in every respect, to the true spirit of our democratical institution" (in Katz 1987, 33). It is not my intention here to argue the merits of democratic localism; I believe this battle continues to be engaged daily in the discourse regarding public education in the United States. Certainly it loomed large in the battles in New York City in 1968 and in Chicago during the early 1990s. Suffice it to say, however, that the schools to which children would be sent were to be organized by the adults in the community. In the educational model proposed by democratic localists, the majority of adults in the community would determine the curriculum and staff for each school. Children's interests were only marginally considered in this model, and the interests of the minorities within the district were wholly ignored. "Orestes Brownson notwithstanding, the people of the Berkshires probably concerned themselves more with the problem of putting orthodox texts in the classroom than with the theory of federalism" upon which democratic localism was based (Katz 1987, 36). Many of the advocates of democratic localism equated education with indoctrination and viewed the schools as the primary agency for achieving this goal. "Certainly, at its worst, democratic localism in action was the tyrannical local majority whose ambition was control and the dominance of their own narrow sectarian or political bias in the schoolroom" (Katz 36). Again, school becomes a construct to which children may be sent and where they may be educated in the mores of adulthood.

Neither did corporate voluntarism nor "the conduct of single institutions as individual corporations, operated by self-perpetuating boards of trustees and financed either wholly through endowment or through a combination of endowment and tuition" (Katz 1987, 37) gain sway in the United States. And again, the controversy focused on the definition of the *public* in public school. Since the schools established in the corporate voluntarist model were not necessarily supported by the public nor founded in a public, they could not be considered public schools. The fight for the common public school doomed this model.

Finally the model that did succeed for the organization of the public schools was that of the bureaucracy. It is a long and involved history told better by historians of education (see Katz 1973, 1987; Nasaw 1979). One critique of democratic localism was that it harkened back in its structures to a country that no longer existed if indeed it ever had; the United States was moving toward an urban culture, and the schools needed to be organized to meet this change. The development of other industrial systems provided first the model and then the need for school bureaucracy. It was deemed necessary to ensure that school attendance be mandatory and regular. This was to minimize the influence of the home and to maximize the socialization effects of the school. Local districts as called for in the democratic localist model could not ensure such attendance. And because these school reformers held such a contemptuous and scornful image of the urban poor, they held that "the primary object" in removing the child from the influence of the parent to the influence of the school was, Henry Barnard would say (in Katz 1987, 44), "not so much . . . intellectual culture, as the regulation of the feelings and dispositions, the extirpation of vicious propensities, the preoccupation of the wilderness of the young heart with the seeds and germs of moral beauty, and the formation of a lovely and virtuous character by the habitual practice of cleanliness, delicacy, refinement, good temper, gentleness, kindness, justice, and truth." These are all values requisite for a smoothly ordered and well-running organization whose values facilitate the functioning of that organization.

Arguing against advocates of democratic localism and one-room schoolhouses organized by the Lancastrian system of education,[10] the proponents of bureaucratic control over schools

---

[10] This was a system established in the paternalistic voluntarism paradigm wherein students were trained to tutor other students, thereby permitting large numbers of children to be educated with a minimum of cost.

argued for the establishment of graded schools where children of different ages would be kept separate for their own protection. They would remain under the watchful eyes of specially trained personnel who themselves would be supervised by specially trained personnel. Again, we see here the development of a conception of childhood and of an education for that conception; furthermore, we see the establishment of a hierarchy endemic to the bureaucratic model for organization. Spatial and temporal concerns became the means for organizing education. Efficiency in educational matters was now de rigueur and was conceptualized as being in the best interests of the child. And this led to administrative offices and professional training. Katz writes that "education had become a difficult and complex undertaking whose conduct and administration demanded the attention of individuals with specialized talents, knowledge, and experience." Of course, this dictum for education assumed something about the child as well.

The social efficiency model of education continued to hold sway throughout the twentieth century as well, and schools therefore took on the structure that facilitated this ideology. Taylorism and the scientific model of curriculum have dominated the schools during the twentieth century. I do not mean to repeat this history. It is a tale oft told. Kliebard argues (1987) that the curriculum has always been the battleground over which different interest groups argued and that throughout the twentieth century the social efficiency model of education has dominated. That model argues that education must be organized based on the needs of the social order and that children must be trained to take their place in it. Franklin Bobbitt (in Kliebard 1987, 98) would write about curriculum:

> Work up the raw material into that finished product for which it is best adapted. Applied to education this means: Educate the individual according to his capabilities. This requires that the materials of the curriculum be sufficiently various to meet the needs of every class of individuals in the community; and that the course of training and study be sufficiently flexible that the individual can be given just the things that he needs.

That is, every child ought to be educated according to his or her place in the social world; efficiency required that educators ought to develop procedures to scientifically assess a child's future role in life and establish curriculum based on those predictions. In a book entitled *Why America's Children Feel Good About Themselves but Can't Read, Write, or Add,* Charles Sykes (1995) argues that the purpose of education is to teach children skills that will be useful to them personally in the marketplace and will also be beneficial collectively to the marketplace. The bureaucratic model of school organization presumes both the need for and efficacy of this efficient organization. Katz (1974, 45-46) writes that "bureaucracy retained the notion of a central monopoly and systematized its operations through the creation of elaborately structured schools and school systems."

Bureaucracy continued and even strengthened the notion that education was something the better part of the community did to the others to make them orderly, moral, and tractable. Thus, an 1876 Report of a Committee on a Course of Study from Primary School to University would write that "It is contended that the public school, being for the masses who are destined to fill the ranks of common laborers, should give a semi-technical education, and avoid disciplinary studies. The latter should be reserved (it is thought) for academies and preparatory schools founded by private enterprise and open to such of the community as can afford to patronize them" (in Willis et al. 1994, 77). This model of educational organization continues to this day. Our children are its victims.

It is a cold morning in early winter. I am still running through the streets of the town. The streets are, of course, quiet. Our children are, of course, in school. And I am oddly enough thinking of another summer and another piper. It is 1965 and my friends and I stand around a car that we should be washing as part of our odd-job business.[11] We do not work very hard: we were lucky to have been born into the middle class, but we needed something to do. We have recently graduated from high school, and we are about to leave for college. Bob Dylan is playing on the ubiquitous radio, this time the one inside the car we are washing.

---

[11] It was odd when we got business and we tended to do it oddly.

Hey! Mr. Tambourine Man, play a song for me,
I'm not sleepy and there is no place I'm going to.
Hey! Mr. Tambourine Man, play a song for me,
In the jingle jangle morning I'll come followin' you.

My friends and I are talking about the identity of Mr. Tambourine Man.[12] Our concerns are real: there is a war going on out there; sex, drugs, and alcohol entice us. We have watched our President be assassinated and his alleged assassin shot to death. It was the summer of the end of our innocence; we wanted our cave back. And Dylan articulated our mute wishes: we were asking the piper to take us away.

Take me on a trip upon your magic swirlin' ship
My senses have been stripped, my hands can't feel to grip,
My toes too numb to step, wait only for my boot heels to be wanderin'
I'm ready to go anywhere, I'm ready for to fade
Into my own parade, cast your dancing spell my way,
I promise to go under it.

I seem to know now, as perhaps I knew then, the identity of this piper, and it is reductionist to label him a drug dealer.[13] Rather, he is portrayed as a deliverer, a way to escape the world be it with drugs or without. He is for me the piper summoned. He is a piper but one whose coming is hailed. You see, the Pied Piper of Hamelin is a tale told by an adult who wishes on one level that the townspeople had not been so greedy; but on another level the tale expresses the unconscious wish for the disappearance of the children. But unlike the children in the Pied Piper, the children in Dylan's "Mr. Tambourine Man" make invitation to this piper asking for relief from this adult world. "Let me forget about today until tomorrow," they plead. The ancient empty streets are too dead for dreaming. That is how I feel as I run this day through my community: the empty streets are too dead for dreaming. We have lost our children. They are in school. It's alright, ma, I'm only bleeding.

---

[12] It is a topic that is addressed in the recent film *Dangerous Minds*. There Dylan's use of code is the focus.

[13] In *Dangerous Minds* it is this hook that enables the teacher to attract students to poetry—the coded messages.

Chapter VIII

The Social Construction
of the Child by the Adult

I stand at the kitchen counter and I prepare my daughter's lunch for the school day. It is 6:00 a.m. and the full moon lights the kitchen counter where I work. I pack her lunch pail (this is her term and not mine—she does not yet know of its usage in the working class mining communities): sandwich, carrot sticks, chips, juice, and dessert. Well balanced, I think. She will eat the chips and the dessert certainly; the sandwich and carrot sticks are doubtful. She claims that "they" don't give her enough time to finish her lunch and she eats slowly! I will make sure she takes her vitamins at breakfast. It is early morning, and the household is still and at peace. I think about her asleep upstairs. I think about her day at school. I think about who and what she is asleep upstairs and who and what she is awake and out at school.

She is a child, and I stand here preparing her midday meal. At school her lunch is scheduled at 11:15 a.m. I hope she will be hungry, but I have my doubts. Why do they ask her to eat her lunch so soon after breakfast? If she doesn't eat her lunch I don't think she will get a snack—that phenomenon usually stops at kindergarten. So too does naptime. Last evening as a family we watched *The Miracle Worker*. As we sat, Emma's hands moved in imitation of the signing so requisite to the opening of Helen's world. I do not think she will have the opportunity to discuss this in school today. How will my daughter's world be opened today? I remember our book reading of the night before: when she comes to a word she doesn't know, she can often substitute a word she does know; but when she tries to sound the word out, she does so a letter name at a time. Do they know that at school? Will they address it soon? How will they do so? In what contexts?

I think about these and many other questions that concern my daughter.[1] I know that I am creating the child upstairs, that is, creating not in the biological sense—that event has long since passed—but in the sociocultural and ideological sense.[2] Who sleeps upstairs has a lot to do with who I think sleeps upstairs and that is in large measure a product of who I think at present is making lunch downstairs. Althusser (1971, 176) says that "Before its birth, the child is therefore always-already a subject, appointed as a subject in and by the specific familial ideological configuration in which it is expected once it has been conceived." Pediatricians T. Berry Brazleton and Bertram Cramer (1990, 15) argue that "A new child is never a total stranger. Parents see in each baby-to-be a possibility of reviving attachments that may have been dormant for years, a new opportunity to work them through. The feelings contained in these previous relationships will once more be played out, in an effort to resolve them." And the child that I create is a product of the lived experience I have not only with her but with my own childhood and that of my parents and they with their parents and so on and so on and so on. If narratives are socially constructed and chart the memory-produced history of self, then doesn't that mean, Mark Freeman (1993, 202) asks, "that we can study [narratives] not only in order to learn about individual selves but about the social realities in which these selves have lived—realities that have indeed become inscribed in their very being?" My child's life is heavily inscribed by the world; I am writing a narrative to help learn about her and her world of school.

What about those adults already in the school? When they think about my child about whom do they think? Are they aware that the children with whom they engage are the complex productions of Althusser's interpellation, or hailing; or Brazleton's expectation; or Freeman's narration, as well as of their own

---

[1] Of course I think about other things as well, but this is only partly autobiographical.

[2] Although in the preparation of her lunch, etc., I might say that I am helping sustain her biological existence.

power to become conscious enough of their world to control their destiny within the historical conditions of their lives. Or will they address these children—my child—as a univocal object of study? David Jardine (1988a, 184) writes eloquently about this concern. Arguing that the dominant (Piagetian) discourse in the study of childhood has created the child as "a univocal object domain with particular characteristics or properties," Jardine asserts that it is thus impossible to hear the child's own voice. Thus constructed, Jardine (1988a, 183) argues, "proper access" to the child for the purposes say, of education, becomes defined "as that method which will express this univocal, objective character, this character of children as they exist apart from the life we live with them, this character of children as they exist apart from the life we see them lead as a feature of everyday life (at home, in school, in children's societies, etc.)." The method is to study the child outside the child's life using the language of an objective scientific discourse. It is to dismiss the child's experience by relegating it to a phase. In this way we falsify the actual lived experience of children and of our lives amidst them (Jardine 1988, 184):

> Piagetian theory begins with a pretense. We must pretend that we do not already understand children in a multitude of interweaving, often contradictory ways, that we do not already understand ourselves to be adults, until the method of genetic epistemology is instigated. We must forget that we already live our lives with children, that we already belong to a culture, a language, a history in which children are already "there all around us." In this pretense of forgetting, we find that anything that does not fall within the purview of scientific discourse must be shunted into the realm of the "personal," the "private," the "biographical" or "autobiographical." We find, in all of this, that issues of adulthood and childhood are handed back to us as the objects of expert advice, child-care manuals, curriculum guidelines, to the extent that it becomes more and more difficult to see how it is possible to be a "good" parent or teacher without recourse to such objectification.

I am sympathetic to Jardine's concerns. What I would like to discuss here is how education has been complicitous in creating the child who becomes the object for Piaget's study and how the child is a product of an adult repression concerning childhood. If as David Jardine (1988a) notes, Piaget's study of the child is made possible because, in Piaget's words, "there are children all around us," then according to Piaget this is so because children "exist apart from us" that they may be studied. "It is against the background of this ontological assumption of the 'being' of children, that the phrase 'there are children all around us' is set out as an answer to questions regarding the field of study for genetic epistemology" (Jardine 1988a, 183). Our study of children, Piaget seems to assume, posits an entity that exists apart from us who are not children and who may be, thus, univocally known. Ignoring our own childhoods, we deny our knowledge of our children.

However, though I believe that children have always existed and have not only recently come into existence, I believe as well that the modern child—the object of Piaget's work—is a particular product of the establishment of formal pedagogical structures that have defined that child. Piaget's study sought the genesis of structures based in the development of adult thought. Indeed, as David Jardine (1988b, 295) writes, we have packed our cognitive abilities into children as well. Arguing that pedagogy has been defined by our idea of the child, Jardine argues as well that our idea of the child arises out of adult notions of cognitive capabilities.

> The children in Piaget's experiment are the progeny of the *cogito* and the inheritors of a picture of the world in which nature has become answerable to the methodical constructions of human understanding. . . . Understanding becomes a matter of construction, and self-understanding, in Piagetian theory, becomes a matter of explicitly setting forth those constructions in terms of objective methodology. Such setting forth houses understanding within the parameters of that which speaks with a common voice, a common understanding. . . . As the object of understanding-as-construction, children are banished to silence.

We have defined children's learning by adult scientific standards; the child comes into being in the discourse of the society of adults as a cognitive organization upon whom pedagogical practices must be enacted to ensure the education of the child. If there is a child outside this conception s/he has been effectively silenced.

What is the connection between education and the child? A more basic question asks, from where does the child come? I do not mean this question in the biological sense of course, but rather in the sociological or sociocultural sense, in the term's social context. For the child as we know it, as it speaks in Dylan's voice, did not always exist. Indeed, the child as a public commentator on adult values may be considered a fairly recent invention, though perhaps we might consider childhood itself as always a comment on adult society. Of course the child almost never speaks except from an adult position; as adults we would not have them bear so blatant witness against us. It is even only in contemporary times that child-narrators such as, say, Huck Finn or Holden Caulfield have spoken. As adults we have, as it were, always unpacked our unconscious into the character of the child. We have created children not only out of our own cognitive beliefs but out of our own emotional needs; we attribute to children emotional capacities based on adult understandings.

Of course, the child must have always existed; every age must have had some concept of children and their childhood, but that concept is always based in the value system maintained by adult society and is not always a unitary construction. Adults discover their own history in the construction of their childhoods; in that process the child is invented as the adult's parent. For example, Michael Lerner (1994) defines the origins of Judaism as deriving from "the psychodynamics of childhood." In Lerner's view, the Hebrew patriarch, Abraham, was the victim of child abuse (a contemporary concept) and his attempts to overcome that abuse and his inability to completely do so display not only the remnants of that abuse (as in the binding of Isaac and the loss of stories other than those of Abraham) but the transcendence of that abuse as well. "We must remember," Lerner (1994, 59) says, "that Abraham's greatness, and the insight that we need to hold on to and build upon, is that ultimately he heard another voice of God, and that second voice allowed him to transcend the past and break the chain of necessity that always threatens to link generations in an embrace of cruelty." Judaism is thus founded on a particular psychology of the abused child. Lerner argues that "The real God of the universe is not the voice of cruelty that [Abraham] had experienced and heard in childhood; it is rather a God of compassion and justice who does not command the sacrifice of the innocent." In Lerner's view, whatever else childhood may be, it is innocent and, therefore, its sociocultural appearance must be understood as a narrative construction of contemporary adult society. God in Lerner's view is that force that makes possible the moment of transcendence and freedom, a breaking free of the repetition compulsion of child abuse. Lerner (1994, 49) posits Judaism as beginning "in the real world, the world of empires and ruling classes and parents who become the instruments for delivering to children the legacy of unresolved pain and hurt." Children are conceptualized as the victims of adult violence and represent the slight possibility for hope for human redemption.

Jesus too, we are told, understood children as innocent, recognizing that the child's pure spirit was the essence of religious life and that the dependence children exhibit is a model for adult relationship to the Deity: "Truly, I say to you unless you turn and become like children, you will never enter the Kingdom of God. Whoever humbles himself like this child, he is the greatest in the Kingdom of God. Whoever receives one such child in my name receives me." Jesus taught that adults must all be as humble as are children, even as adults must care for children because of their vulnerability.

Of course this attitude was markedly in contrast to the dominant Western view of children during Jesus' time. At best, Richard Lyman, Jr. (1974, 81) writes, it is probable that the more prevalent attitude concerning children during the Roman era was that they were "really something of a bother." It was perhaps not until Rousseau that children retrieved that innocence posited by Jesus that they have not yet lost.[3] The Greeks and Romans held that the child did not have adult cognitive capacities; a child does not reason and therefore its thinking was defective even though it might *appear* faultless as a result of this inadequacy. That innocence, unlike in Jesus' teachings, was hardly a model for adult attitudes. Education, then, should teach proper thinking. Aristotle would write that "No one would choose to live with the intellect of a child throughout his life, however much he were to be pleased at the things that children are pleased at, nor to get enjoyment by doing some dis-

---

[3] For an alternative view of the child see Joe Kincheloe, "Home Alone" in *Kinderculture*, forthcoming.

graceful deed, though he were never to feel any pain in consequence" (in Boas 1966, 13). The chief characteristic of the child
in this formulation was that it was not an adult. Rather, the
child was not a particular adult—one who thought in forms
deemed suitable by those who could determine correctness.

Children are, of course, what happens to procreative adults,
and the experiences children have are called childhood. But of
what that childhood might consist is always determined by the
adult society. What remains for our narrative of childhood is
finally the work of adults who talk about children and the social attitudes that exist toward them. Gerald Graff writes (1995,
6) that "outside discourse . . . there is no 'child,' no 'adolescence,' no one 'childhood' or 'adolescence,' nor is there a 'family.'" Rather, as Graff's history attempts to show, there are distinct patterns of growing up in specific historical circumstances;
childhood becomes defined by the history of these patterns.
Historians of childhood are clear that our present notion of
the child is an ideological construct that derives from particular social conditions. The *Oxford English Dictionary* notes that
the word "child" refers in the Bible to any male entering man-
hood but that subsequently and for the most part "child" refers to female progeny much more than to male offspring, and
that childhood is defined as the state of being a child: from
birth to puberty. As I will show, this latter description refers to
merely physical characteristics and offers no clue as to the attributes that attach to "childhood." Indeed, as Lyman (1974,
77) points out, during the Roman era "the term 'child' seems
to refer to anyone, depending on context and literary conven-
tion, from infancy to old age."

The term "child" is a signifier out of which meaning must
be produced. Joseph Kett (1977, 36) notes that in the United
States during the eighteenth century the word 'child' referred
to all pupils at school. He writes that "If childhood is defined
as a period of protected dependency within the home, then its
extent was much shorter then than now. If adolescence was
defined as the period after puberty during which a young person is institutionally segregated from casual contacts with a
broad range of adults, then it can scarcely be said to have existed at all, even for those young people who attended school
beyond age 14." The child was more a product of physical con-

ditions than it was a psychological entity; social customs regarding dependency, work, and so on determined the substance, character, and experience of the child. Although the
child in all its complex and individualized stages—infant, child,
preteen, adolescent, postadolescent—derives from the twentieth century and even may be traced in its development to the
last fifty years, since the end of World War II, I believe that the
actual origin of the modern child predates this century by several hundred years and might be associated with the formal
development of schools.

Neil Postman argues that what he understands as the preoccupation with the history of childhood is already a sign that it
is on its wane. "At the very least," Postman (1994, 4) writes,
"we may say that the best histories of anything are produced
when an event is completed, when a period is waning, when it
is unlikely that a new and more robust phase will occur." I do
not believe childhood is disappearing; rather, I assert that its
definitions are changing and that these definitions are tied to
the growth of the modern school.

Postman claims that a sense of shame was necessary for the
invention of childhood. It is adults, however, who feel shame,
and they must hide from the children that about which shame
is felt. Distinguishing between shame and guilt, John Murray
Cuddihy (1974, 59) states: "Shame is a 'condition' rather than
an action . . . shame is an exposure, not a deed." In this sense,
children become those before whom certain acts must not be
displayed.[4] It is not the act but its display that must be concealed and then only from a select population—in this case,
from children. Schools were organized to remove children from
adult society and avert adult shame. Now, schools were also,
Postman (1994, 36) writes, where reading might be learned,
and therefore reading matter—curriculum—becomes implicated
in adult shame; reading pedagogy is organized to define what
children may read. "From print onward," Postman (36) writes,
"the young would have to *become* adults, and they would have to
do it by learning to read, by entering the world of typogra-

---

[4] Jonathan Silin (1995) writes on a related theme when he discusses the
avoidance of AIDS and death in the curriculum of childhood.

phy." Hence, adults could avoid shame by denying certain readings to what they would deem as children. Rousseau would later argue that keeping children from this early pedagogy was essential for the child's education. Schools and the pedagogy they offered protected adults from shame to which children might expose them.

C. John Sommerville (1987) suggests that the first actual "schools" may have been established among the Hebrews; with the Temple destroyed, Judaism could no longer be attached to place and became a religion of the Book, so to speak. We have few records of what occurred in these schools, but it seems clear that the education practiced there concerned indoctrination into the laws by an exegetical style that focused on interpretation of the Book. Of course the ability to read was essential. But as I have said elsewhere (Block 1995, 5), "The way one is taught to read becomes the purpose and manner of reading: the technique becomes the thing." The child was educated not only as the adult but to be the adult as well.

Lloyd deMause (1974) argues that the history of childhood must be conceptualized by the psychogenic theory of history. This theory argues that the history of humanity must be conceptualized as deriving from the "psychogenic changes in personality occurring because of successive generations of parent-child interactions" (deMause 1974, 3). Unlike Lerner, deMause (1974, 1) sees in the history of childhood an evolution of adult behavior with children that represents "a nightmare from which we have only recently begun to awaken." DeMause argues that because psychic structure is always passed from generation to generation through the narrow funnel of childhood, a society's child-rearing practices are not just one item in a list of cultural traits. Rather, these traits comprise means for the transmission and development of all other cultural elements. Of course, deMause understands evolution as a linear progression and that the history of childhood represents a progressive development in child care: children become defined by how they are treated. "The origin of this evolution lies in the ability of successive generations of parents to regress to the psychic age of their children and work through the anxieties of that age in a better manner the second time they encounter them than they did during their own childhood."

As does Lerner, deMause situates his history of childhood in the psychology of adults.

I think deMause's theory is flawed in several respects. According to his view the evolution of childhood depends on the development of psychic structures in adulthood that permit better care to be taken of their children. But it is clear that deMause reads back into history using psychological categories that arise out of a contemporary historical setting. He attributes the treatment of children to undeveloped psychic structures and posits progress in child care to a psychoanalytic model. What provokes that change is not part of his essay. Indeed, deMause (1974, 3) argues that "this generational pressure" for psychic change takes place not only spontaneously "but also occurs independent to social and technological change." For deMause, the history of childhood seems strangely enough ahistorical.

Furthermore, deMause (1974, 3) argues that "the history of childhood is a series of closer approaches between adult and child, with each closing of psychic distance producing fresh anxiety. The reduction of this adult anxiety is the main source of the child-rearing practices of each age." However, deMause does not ascribe a locus whence that anxiety might arise except from an *a priori* view of the child vis à vis the adult and organized by some ideal notion of the child. Furthermore, deMause seems to have organized this rapprochement as moving inevitably toward a merging of child and adult: as we quit abusing children we must inevitably cease abusing adults. To my mind deMause situates childhood in an ideal of the child that might itself be understood in its historical setting but from which the actual situation in history has been removed.

Other historical studies (Ariès 1965) have shown that the contemporary child is an ideological invention that developed between the thirteenth and the seventeenth centuries and that can be directly linked to the development of the educational establishment over that time period. More directly, the child was the invention of the educational mechanism of which the child became the primary object and project. Hence, education and the child are inseparable entities; notions of the former are organized by understandings of the latter, and what is important for my study here, the opposite is also true: how the child is conceptualized is dependent on a conceptualization of education. It is to these studies that I now turn.

The Invention of the Child

Prior to the thirteenth century, neither education nor the child as we know it existed. Rather, people held to a belief in what might be called the "ages of man." This belief was based upon a conception of Nature as a unitary and continuous whole of which human existence was a part. Thus, ages were organized by numbers of years that corresponded to a natural growth cycle, sometimes even corresponding to the months of the year, but to which no psychological character was attached. January was young but not cold nor immature. December was old but not bitter. Our contemporary mythologies regarding the new year continue this portrait of childhood as a merely physical condition. Childhood merely marked a period of dependency; when that dependency was over—it could last for as few as seven years or as many as thirty years—the individual entered adulthood. A day and an activity distinguished these two periods; no other attributes separated the child from the adult. Cultural historian, Phillipe Ariès (1965, 23), notes that "life for men of old . . . was the inevitable, cyclical sometimes amusing and sometimes sad continuity of the ages of life; a continuity inscribed in the general and abstract order of things rather than in real experience, for in those periods of heavy mortality, few men were privileged to live through all the ages." But these ages, regardless of who lived through them, had no psychological coloration attached to them: they were merely a quantitative measurement of years to which qualitative assessment would be affixed. In *Le Grand Propriétarire de toute choses*, a medieval text that deals with the ages of man, this is how the first four stages are described (in Ariès 1965, 210):

> The first age is childhood when the teeth are planted, and this age begins when the child is born and lasts until seven, and in this age that which is born is called an infant, which is as good as saying not talking, because in this age it cannot talk well or form its words perfectly for its teeth are not yet well arranged or firmly planted. . . . After infancy comes the second age . . . it is called *pueritia* and is given this name because in this age the person is still like the pupil in the

eye . . . and this age lasts till fourteen. . . . After follows the third age, which is called adolescence, which ends according to Constantine, in the twenty-first year, but according to Isidore it lasts till twenty-eight . . . and it can go on till thirty or thirty-five. . . . Afterwards follows youth, which occupies the central position among the ages, although the person in this age is in his greatest strength, and this lasts until forty-five according to Isidore. This age is called youth because of the strength in the person to help himself and others.

We ought to note first that the terms *childhood, infant, pueritia, adolescence,* and *youth* do not in any way correspond to our modern understanding of those terms. Second, we must recognize that the ages are linked to the cycle of physical nature, a universal and unswerving force over which humans could have very little control. Both points suggest to us that our contemporary view of the child rests on somewhat immediate assumptions: first, that the child has special *psychological* characteristics that separate it from other defined age categories; and second, that those characteristics are linked linearly to a progress of development through which every human must pass to achieve a socially accepted adulthood. Childhood, for us, is understood as a psychological state through which an individual must successfully progress in order to become a productive adult human being. That passage is socially defined; thus, there are certain capacities of the child, particular to a specific age, that may be fashioned into desired form—may be acted upon by those who have defined those capacities as being precedent to the characteristics of the adult. Seen in this light, childhood in the contemporary world may be understood as a product of adult repression: *we impose on the child those characteristics we adults would desire and cannot have ourselves.*

To effect this construction, we invent and conceptualize experiences that we may then organize to fashion that form. But in medieval ideology (by which word I mean a complex system of signifying practices and symbolic processes in a particular society such that these practices and processes comprise reality, which cannot be conceived outside those beliefs), up to about the thirteenth century, the belief in the "ages of man" made the attempt to alter development unthinkable. After all, there is little need to exert influence over any aspect of natural existence because nature is by definition unsubmissive to human will. Learning and education were routinely understood by these people to be a natural part of existence for most of the population. What formal education did exist prepared men for the priesthood but did not define its audience other than by gender. Pedagogy was geared toward a body of knowledge and not toward the development of character. Education was organized by the requirements of religious ideologies: "The instruction was therefore essentially professional or technical . . . the pupils learned what they needed to know in order to say and sing the offices, namely the Psalms and the canonic Hours, in Latin of course, the Latin of the manuscripts in which these texts had been established" (Ariès 1965, 138). Education functioned to one end: the production of a priestly order. For the most part, this education was ecclesiastical and age did not enter as a factor. In this educational environment the curriculum was not graded nor were certain subjects offered at various times for different age groups. The simultaneity of the curriculum and the absence of a graded structure were salient features of medieval education. Indeed, all ages were mixed together in the same classroom in the medieval school. But as Ariès reminds us, even to note this is to place a modern perspective on events. There were no children in the medieval school: childhood *as we know it* had not yet been invented. Primary education did not exist in the medieval world: reading, writing, and education in the mother tongue all took place at home or within an apprenticeship to a trade. A reading knowledge of Latin was the only academic requirement needed for admission to the arts course [in the medieval university], the basic course of study.

The centrality of the Church in the development of the school is important to note: prior to the fifth century, the Church had trusted the Hellenistic schools to teach their students literary knowledge required for the reading of the Bible and the commentaries. But as the Church viewed Hellenistic culture as depraved, and as that particular culture indeed began to decay, the Church assumed more and more the responsibility for education in such subjects. Education was necessary: priests were required to have what we would call literary knowledge, the knowledge of the sacred texts; to have artistic knowledge that they could know the plain-song, the prayers;

and to know scientific knowledge, mostly of astronomy, that they would know how to compute the occurrence of Easter. As rural life declined and as the rise of urban centers increased their importance, those persons training for religious orders were educated within the large cathedral churches by their elders who taught them mostly by rote: prayers were repeated in unison until they were memorized. "The priests could recite nearly all the prayers in their office from memory. Henceforth, reading was no longer an indispensable tool of learning. It served to aid their memory in the event of forgetfulness" (in Ariès 1965, 138).[5] It is interesting to note that memorization was the dominant educational method; to a large extent this educational practice still exists today.

But equally relevant to our purposes here is to note that the curriculum was yet ungraded and simultaneous: all students sat in the class together and received all the information. There was no distinction in age. And still the majority of children—even those of the more well-to-do—were not sent to school for their education but to the homes of others where they served apprenticeships of various sorts, waiting tables, for example, until they had developed the capacity to live independently. What must be noted is that education took place amongst society and not, as today, apart from it. Education in the medieval world was integral to practice in the world. And for the education of specific populations, such as the priesthood, there was no age discrimination within the educational forum: "I saw the students in the school. . . . Their numbers were great. . . . I saw there men of diverse ages: *pueros, adolescentes, juvenes, senes* . . ." (in Ariès 1965, 153). There was no word to denote an adult: one went from youth to old age.

Now, it is only after an aspect of Nature can be isolated that it can be influenced: hence, it is only after the invention of

---

[5] Postman (1994, 36) argues that it was the printing press--the invention of reading--that made childhood possible. "What had happened, simply, was that Literate Man had been created. And in his coming, he left behind the children. For in the medieval world neither the young nor the old could read, and their business was in the here and now. . . . That is why there had been no need for the idea of childhood, for everyone shared the same information environment and therefore lived in the same social and intellectual world."

childhood that attempts can be made to develop in it certain characteristics. This latter attempt is the practice of education under the guidance of predominantly moral ideologues and churchmen. "There can be no doubt," Ariès (1965, 43) declares, "that the importance accorded to the child's personality was linked with the growing influence of Christianity on life and manners." Phrased another way, the invention of childhood is a product of education that itself develops in a hierarchical, perfectly ordered, and controlled system. Under the influence of the Church, education since the thirteenth century, except in rare occasions such as Summerhill, the Deweyan model school, or the Modern School Movement of the twentieth century (see Avrich 1980), has always been the invention and the imposition of discipline. And discipline (Foucault 1979) is the practice of power that is not acquired by a dominant class but is rather exercised as a result of its strategic positioning. This distinction is important: power is not imposed on a particular population; rather, power creates that population. Education controls the child, but first it must invent that child. Discipline, the organizing principle of the modern educational system, is the product of the exercise of power by moral pedagogues and churchmen and results from their strategic position in a specific society. It is through discipline that childhood will come into being replete with characteristics that can then be developed.

The theocentrism of the medieval world and the continuing centrality of church authority placed certain pedagogues in a position to exercise power. Power produces reality; it *creates* reality. The individual being comes into existence when it is defined, and it is defined by how it is written and constructed. Aries' book portrays in part how churchmen in the theocentric world of the thirteenth, fourteenth, and fifteenth centuries organized from the undisciplined and unstructured educational system that existed prior to their efforts the authoritarian and hierarchical government of the colleges from which the modern primary and secondary school developed in an unbroken line of continuing imposition of discipline. Starting in the fifteenth century and as a result of schooling, education became the normal instrument of social initiation, of progress from childhood to adulthood. This evolution corresponded to the

pedagogues' desire for moral severity, to their concern to isolate youth from the corrupt world of adults, and to their determination to train the child to resist adult temptations. These
pedagogues were almost always church officials: indeed, the
humanist scholars, to whom are usually attributed the development of modern education, continued to argue that an ideal
education ought to extend throughout life, beyond childhood
and adolescence whose character and existential nature they
could not distinguish.

But the churchmen and moral pedagogues had arrived at a
definition of the child as innocent and therefore in need of
protection from a corrupted world; as weak because of that
innocence and therefore a moral responsibility to the masters.
Education conceptualized as a training of the child became
based on these beliefs and is the work predominantly of church
ideology. The moral solicitude toward children evident in the
philosophy and behavior of the churchmen and moral ideologues made them eager *for the child's own good* to instill disciplined and rational manners. These men recognized in children a fragility that required safeguarding and reforming. Thus,
where the mother would usually "coddle" the infant child, developing church ideology pointed out the deleterious effects
such behavior would have on the moral growth of the child:
"Every man must be conscious of that insipidity of childhood
which disgusts the sane mind; that coarseness of youth which
finds pleasure in scarcely anything but material objects and
which is only a very crude sketch of the man of thought" (in
Ariès 1965, 131). Needless to say, that development could only
be undertaken away from the bad influence of the home and
certainly away from the world that was not innocent or weak,
as was the conceptualized child. In these attitudes begins the
development of the modern school.

Not that education was absent from the medieval world, but
the control over the students engaged in education was established by those interested in guarding and protecting them.
The Christian religious establishment, in opposition to the students' traditional customs of friendship and self-government
in the medieval world of regular commerce and engagement
with the daily world in which they lived, represented an outlook that was "technical, technocratic, Cartesian [in spirit and

characterized by] a love of order, regularity, classification, hierarchy, [and] organization" (Ariès 1965, 252). In short, these churchmen instituted a system that invented the modern school and, concurrently, the modern child. That system was premised on the notion of discipline: a strategic position of control and definition from which power can be exercised.

The perception of the world from which children ought to be protected invented the very children needing custodial care, and to effect this invention, discipline was developed. Now, discipline defines the relations one body must have with an object that that body manipulates. Think of the discipline of weight training and how that discipline defines the relationship a body has with the weight equipment. Think how the discipline defines the body builder. The same is true for the relationship between the church masters and moral ideologues and the bodies they manipulated; in defining relations they defined the bodies as well. I do not mean to suggest that a cadre of men in a secluded chapel conspired in developing these ordering principles to create childhood. Rather, these disciplinary principles developed coincident with the notion of the innocent and weak (weak because innocent) child; these standards grew alongside the very idea of the child. Recall that one cannot influence anything that cannot be first isolated: the practice of discipline invented the reality it was meant to control.

The elements of discipline were premised on three principles. Note how these principles define the body they are meant to manipulate. The first principle included constant supervision, which organized the spatial and temporal world of the incipient child into carefully defined and controlled compartments. From this practice schools would develop in which students were boarded and supervised by school officials, where students' behaviors were carefully regulated and organized, where curricula were developed based on perceived intellectual and psychological capabilities, and in which graded class structure was developed to segregate children at various levels to ensure purity of development.

The second principle concerned the practice of informing raised to a level of institution and principle of government. As school populations increased, constant watch by the masters became impossible. Hence, the development of self-regulation permitted the continuance of disciplinary order in the absence of the school authority. Whereas once students had regulated themselves by the election of peers drawn from their own ranks in free election, children were now considered incapable of behaving themselves without supervision. Henceforth, rules and order were designed by the masters, and if students were to have leaders drawn from their own ranks, they were to be appointed by those above, establishing a hierarchical system instituted by discipline and subject to outside control. Older students were given responsibility to oversee younger ones, defining childhood not only by ages but by behaviors and psychological characteristics. The effects of this practice led to the definitions of certain behaviors, the subsequent internalization of those behaviors by individuals, and the control of those individuals by specific groups with the avowed purpose of shaping behavior. Childhood could now be defined by certain behaviors that could be controlled and developed by a regimen of discipline. To this effect, the third principle of discipline was established: the extension of corporal punishment. Students could now be beaten into obedience.

These elements of discipline were an attempt to protect and to govern, to isolate and instruct. Of course, there must be something to instruct, which posits a particular character that can be changed by and through education, the exercise of the discipline. Indeed, education became the primary social instrument for the governance of the very child it invented. "The argument for schools is that they provide a necessary bridge from childhood to adult life, that they gradually transform the indulged child into the responsible adult" (Reimer 1971, 53). Hence, rather than leave students free to live in the world unsupervised and in direct contact with the diurnal world, the colleges that were first instituted as merely hostels where students lived together and from which students would travel to schools, became gradually controlled by the principles of the religious establishment who began to order the daily lives of the residents—students.

A close watch must be kept on the children, and they must never be left alone anywhere whether they are ill or in good health. . . . This constant supervision should be exercised gently and with a certain trustfulness calculated to make them think that one loves them, and that it is only to enjoy their company that one is with them. This makes them love this supervision rather than fear it (in Ariès 1965, 115).

And as they began to supervise living conditions, not without revolt I would add, for student revolts are integral to the development of discipline, the masters began to organize curricula based on their perceptions of appropriateness of material. Even the gradual disappearance of physical punishment, which historically we are told is practiced only on the poor and helpless, the latter characteristic being consistent with the definition of children from the thirteenth century onward, is ultimately premised not on humanitarian principle. Rather, the elimination of corporal punishment was rationalized on the belief that what is required for obedience is not to beat the child into his/her submission but to awaken in the child notions of adult responsibility and dignity. This education for adult life could not be effected by one brutal stroke, but would occur by careful gradual conditioning—whence, the notion of the graded school, of sequential curricula, of separation by age. And once we have created discipline, we have defined the order. Childhood has been brought into existence by this strategic imposition of order. Ariès' book portrays the undergraduate of the fourteenth century developing from a free gentleman to a mere schoolboy. Education invents the child and it invents him/her through the imposition of discipline.

Thus it is possible to say that education is the institution to which responsibility can be assigned for effecting the construction of the child, because the school is the institution that grew commensurate with the notion of childhood and, therefore, defined it by the school's activities. And what the school invented was the notion of the difference between the child and the rest of society, of the held concept of the innocence and weakness of the child, and the need for its development to survive in the powerful and corrupt world populated already by the adult. Education was organized as an attempt to influence the development of the student. The progress of educational institutions is a progress in the invention of the child by the imposition of discipline.

What is the result of this imposition of discipline? We must first note that childhood becomes the repository of innocence that a severely repressed world felt it had lost. Schiller will say that "Children are what we were" (in Boas 1966, 73). Children are theorized as separate from adults, and what marks that separation is the attribution of certain psychological characteristics particular to the child. Children thus bear the burden for our repression: they must correspond to so narrow a definition that none can finally accommodate. Childhood becomes coincident with adult neurosis and is, thus, organized to act by and in a world that does in fact exist. The establishment of education, then, was organized by this neurotic impulse; the structure that results not only must bear the marks of the violence of which neurosis is capable but must contain as its organizing principle that very violence. John Stuart Mill has written (in Sommerville 1987, 228):

> If the government would make up its mind to *require* for every child a good education, it might save itself the trouble of *providing* one. . . . A general State education is a mere contrivance for moulding people to be exactly like one another: and as the mould in which it casts them is that which pleases the predominant power in the government, whether this be a monarch, priesthood, an aristocracy, or the majority of the existing generation in proportion as it is efficient and successful, it establishes a despotism over the body.[6]

State-organized education is an attempt to create what we have repressed in ourselves. But this act is an act of violence as we attempt to make our dreams the mold for the lives of others. Its result can only be truncated and damaged lives. I would like to discuss briefly how the educational establishment has enacted not merely in Mills' words a despotism over the body forcing it into a set shape, but how that same despotism fashions and subjugates, subjugates by fashioning the child's mind as well. I will argue that the separation of mind and body upon which the school is premised alienates the child from himself and the world and is a violence that is ultimately irreparable in the contemporary world and leads to a form of madness.

---

[6] For a Marxist interpretation of this process, see my essay "Marxism and Education" (1994).

Discipline and the World

We have seen how the child was the invention of the educational system and how the educational system derives from the establishment of discipline. We must now look briefly at what the imposition of discipline might mean to those subject to it; for that discipline creates not only the student but the world in which the student/child exists, creates what activity is and is not deemed possible. And we must examine what it is that we mean by physical and mental health and the role that education might play in the development of both forms of well-being. What effect does the discipline of education have on the development of the child? How may education be understood as implicated in acts of social violence against the child—indeed, how has education created the child as an act of social violence? These are issues that I will address now.

Discipline, as we have seen, is separation. By its actions discipline defines entities, establishes boundaries, and organizes forms. Now, forms as singular entities are specified by outlines and represent separation. Forms are separate objects made so by outlines. In separating one entity from another, outlines in essence create those entities. Now what is perceived as separate is forever lost to us as part of ourselves. It, the form, is not of "I" but of "the other." Our fealty to outlines affirms our belief in an external, solid, permanent world that is not of us but is, rather, separate from us. Outlines confirm us as individual entities by their act of separation, but they also insist on our alienation in that confirmation. We are the other of the other. In her book *On Not Being Able to Paint* (1990) Marion Milner explores the significance of outlines because her inability to paint seems tied directly to her relationship to outlines and to the objects they create. Milner relates how, in painting, her productions appeared either as counterfeit when she attempted to paint representationally (i.e., to follow the outline she saw) or appeared as different from what she had intended when she drew only from her thoughts. When she considered the nature of her failure to represent her vision, it was to her relationship to outlines that she ascribed primary responsibility for the inadequacy. It was, after all, outlines that in their representation matched neither the external reality nor her internal mood. Not being able to paint resulted from the inability to either affirm outline or deny it. The inability to paint seemed to result from an inability to form a relationship between the external and the internal world.

For Milner, painting is the attempt to represent a piece of the world on canvas, but what that world might actually be is called into question by her inability to paint it—by a perceived absence of creativity. Whenever Milner defines her subject prior to painting she seems unable to paint, and the inability to paint despite a technical skill and her desire to do so argues another explanation for her failure. Milner explores *not* being able to paint. This exploration—the engagement in learning how to do so—becomes for her a study of the relationships that create subject and object, self and world, and is a question of outlines and of the discipline that forms them. Painting by its nature—the desire to represent on canvas or some other medium—seems to have something to do with feelings aroused by the idea of space and time, and hence ideas of separation. Painting has to do with outlines: "So it became clear," Milner (1990, 12) writes, "that if painting is so concerned with problems of being a separate body in a world of other bodies which occupy different bits of space, in fact, it must be deeply concerned with ideas of distance and separation and having and losing." Her inability to paint might be understood as a failure to negotiate feelings of distance and separation, of having and losing. These are issues central to existence. Thus, her inability to paint seemed not to stem from a lack of technical skill but resulted rather from conflicted thought about the human condition: of issues regarding separation and loss and the concerns about her capacity as an individual to negotiate those feelings. This felt incapacity became a question of boundaries, of outlines, for it is they that separate and establish distance.

Milner expresses interest in the notion of the outline and its effect on her. Outlines establish the object and offer the illusion that the object is real. Painting may be understood as the drawing of outline: of getting it right. But in close observation, Milner discovers that outlines—which appear as the object of painting and that which create forms that are the painting—are not, as one is led to believe, real: "When really looked at in relation to each other . . . outlines were not clear and compact, as I had always supposed them to be, they continually became lost in shadow" (1990, 15). Try sometime to see an outline of an Other without also seeing its immediate context, its ecology, and you will understand what Milner means: the reality of the solidity of objects dissipates and the separation between world and self begins to dissolve. And when forms break up, fear of madness rises as separation between the world and self vanishes, as what is inside begins to bubble up and threatens the solidity of the external world.

Let us review briefly the importance of the outline. Of what does it remind us? Outlines represent the world of fact, of separate touchable objects; to cling to outlines is to cling to the distinction between self and other, here and there, now and then. Outlines organize spatial and temporal relationships in this world by identifying separateness. Now what is the alternative? If indeed, outlines do not exist, then objects are not fact but are our constructions, and reality is not *there* but is established by a subject in relationship to objects. What we see is what we create; perception is not the beginning of consciousness but the result of it. But this means that in the creation of the object—what is out there—the subject is also constructed, for everything out there is my own construction.

This is the situation Milner explores in order to realize the ability to paint—to be creative—to invent the world and herself. There were spiritual issues: seeing was an act of the imagination. Seeing the outlines of things was difficult; seeing the inside of things was even more profound and frightening. Her inability to paint represented an inability to negotiate these fears and terrors. To attempt to paint representationally, realistically, by drawing outlines is impossible because any view of any object is always fortuitous. "The present moment view of any object is always determined by accident of where one is standing at the moment. . . . To know the truth of people you have to select and combine . . . to combine all the partial glimpses into a relevant whole. This requires imagination." (1990, 14). Hence the world is not real in the sense that it exists outside of us and we must discover it; rather, it is a construction of our imagination, all that we have within us from all past relationships with that which is outside of us whether they were realized as outside relationships or not. Reality, it would seem, derives not from outline, from separation, but in our creation of the world, in our recognition that it is our own construction that establishes objects by our relation to them. Living is a process of relationships; experience is the interplay of vital forces, the activity of relating constantly leading through fresh relatings to a new activity. Our activity changes as we engage in it and does not evolve from purpose to deed and from deed to purpose as if life moved on a pulley with only an "external wire puller to account for the jerks" (Milner 1990, 87). I am a runner not because I own running shoes but because I wear them on the road. I am a runner not because I think about roads but because I run on them. And I am a runner because I run and not because I am finished running. Reality is created in engagement with it, and this occurs in a relational act of construction between our imaginations and that part of the world that makes itself available to our actions. After all, if outlines do not in fact exist, whatever form we see is a product of those outlines we create based on our own needs, wishes, and dreams. "The substance of experience," Milner (1990, 27) attests, "is what we bring to what we see, without our own contribution we see nothing." The power to endow the world with our dreams is creativity. Our action creates the world, and then it is *our* world and not that of common sense.

However, this world that does not coincide with the world of common sense threatens our belief in a common sense reality, threatens belief in our sanity, and is summarily rejected. The belief in outlines staves off the madness that we fear would result by losing our hold on the solid earth. Madness is what we fear by the loss of separateness that would result from the dissolution of outlines. Outlines represent the world of fact; belief in them protects one against the world of the imagination, but it protects at great price. If we accept our role in the creation of objects then those objects cannot be separate from us. But to accept outlines is to endure separation and loss, an extremely painful condition. And so, Milner wonders, and as I wonder now, how is it possible to have remained so long unaware of this fact concerning outlines? Why does it take such a great mental effort to see the edges of objects as they actually show themselves rather than as they are always thought of in the common sense view of reality? From where does that common sense view derive? Do you begin to see the direction in which we head?

Where did we first acquire this fear of the imagination? Well I believe to a large extent it occurs in school. First, we must understand imagination to be the creative impulse, and what we finally create is ourselves. How is this? As in painting, experience is the establishment of a dialogic relationship between the external world and our own wishes and dreams. In painting, that relationship establishes a picture; in life, it establishes experience. The world is blank until we create it—paint it. A painting is never reality but merely one's creation of it: after all, isn't there always something outside the framed canvas? Isn't a painting only something held in by a frame? Creativity is a reciprocal relationship between what is inside—dreams— and what is outside. To learn to paint is to learn how to endow the objects of the external world with a spiritual life, "action," that is appropriate to their nature. One seeks, says Milner, to find a bit of the outside world that is willing to temporarily fit in with one's dream.[7] In that illusion occurs a moment in which the inner and outer seem to coincide, in which a unity is achieved and world and self are one and of our creation. It is in those moments that one begins to believe in the life of action, a life in which one could seek to rebuild, restore, and recreate what one loved in actual achievement. In creativity we come to understand that the outside world actually wants what we have to give; we fill the gap by creating the gap. In painting, we deliberately restore the split between subject and object and bring together the two into a new unity. In painting the world is altered, distorted from its natural shape to fit the inner experience. One becomes whole. We are the world.

The discipline of school that has invented children denies the act of creation and in that denial commits an execrable act of social violence. For to deny imagination is to deny the very creativity that makes self possible; it is to perpetuate the hate that results from the inescapable discrepancy between subjective and objective, between the unlimited possibilities of one's dream and what the real world actually offers us. To deny imagination is to instill hatred where should stem love and creativity. For hate must be the result of the conflict between our

---

[7] Recall that Winnicott said that the good enough parent was one who would not be destroyed.

dreams and the world that condemns and denies those dreams. The school that is structured by and about boundaries makes painting impossible and makes us hate ourselves for our thought-dreams. In school's denial of the dialogic relationship that permits painting (and I use painting as the metaphor for creating experience), the school establishes a dictatorship over the child in which reality is defined by the other. World and self are made separate and the imagination—the wishes and dreams—are denied for the predetermined outlines of the other. This violence denies the very existence of the individual child and denies that child all opportunity to learn. Learning is, after all, the ability to change: as we paint, the cause of the primary hate is lessened as we enrich the inner world in relationship with the outer world, and we have less cause of despair of ever finding anything that can accommodate our dreams. In the act of creation, a bit of the outside world is distorted, twisted into shape to fit our inner experience, but we have labored to make that piece of the outside world nearer our inner conception, not in the way of the practical work of the world, but in our own fashion and according to our own dreams.

But the denial of this possibility—the act of violence perpetrated by the school—demands that the individual respond in certain protective ways. The child is formed as a result of violence and within the regime of school practices is maintained by violence. The child is denied hope of establishing creative and healthy relationships. As a result of this despair he/she may become a dictatorial egoist who actively denies the wishes and needs of the other (and this may include the physical earth as well as other people) and tries to make his/her own wishes alone determine what happens. Here is one who wholly denies the demands of an external world. Or one may become a passive egoist, retreating from public reality and taking refuge in a world of unexpressed dreams, becoming remote and inaccessible. Read Willa Cather's *Paul Case* to find a vivid portrayal of this result. Or finally, to avoid conflict, the individual may permit the outside world to become a dictator, may fit him/herself into that external world and its demands and result in doing what others want and betraying his/her own wishes and dreams.

The act of social violence that the school commits against the child is a product of the very nature of the school, which itself has invented the contemporary view of childhood. But in that design (which will not go away any more than the discovery of nuclear energy can be obliterated) we have practiced social violence upon the child. As schools were created by the establishment of discipline, they have created their objects by that very discipline. They deny painting, deny imagination, and ultimately deny learning.

I want to conclude this chapter by returning to Bob Dylan. As he has articulated my despair, he also gives voice to my hope. Having suffered from the violence the world has practiced on him as a child, he has struggled his way through to a vision of health. And it is not accidental that health occurs in creativity, in the establishment of relationships between the world and the I, between subject and object, and that this occurs in the act of painting.

> Oh the hours I've spent inside the Colosseum,
> Dodging lions and wastin' time.
> Oh, those mighty kings of the jungle, I could hardly stand to see 'em
> Yes, it sure has been a long, hard climb
> . . . .
> Someday, everything is gonna be smooth like a rhapsody
> When I paint my masterpiece.

Until we create an environment in which the child may use the educational establishment to create him or her self, until we serve only as frame on which the canvas may appear in paint, we will continue to practice extreme violence upon the child, denying him/her growth, health, and experience.

References

Althusser, L. 1971. *Lenin and Philosophy*. B. Brewster, Trans., New York: Monthly Press.

Ariès, P. 1965. *Centuries of Childhood*. New York: Vintage.

Astington, J. W. 1993. *The Child's Discovery of the Mind*. Cambridge: Harvard Univ. Press.

Avrich, P. 1980. *The Modern School Movement: Anarchism and Education in the United States*. Princeton: Princeton Univ. Press.

Bauman, Z. 1991. *Ambivalence and Modernity*. Ithaca: Cornell Univ. Press.

Block, A. A. 1994. "Marxism and Education." In R. Martusewicz and W. Reynolds, Eds., *Inside/Out: Contemporary Perspectives in Education*. New York: St. Martin's.

———. *Occupied Reading*. New York: Garland.

———, and Klein, S. 1996. "Having a Wonderful Time, Wish You Were Here: Walking, Postcards and Curriculum." *Art Education*. 49(3): 20-24.

Boas, G. 1966. *The Cult of Childhood*. Dallas: Spring Publications.

Bollas, C. 1987. *The Shadow of the Object*. New York: Columbia Univ. Press.

———. 1989. *Forces of Destiny*. New York: Columbia Univ. Press.

———. 1992. *Being a Character*. New York: Hill and Wang.

Brazleton, T. B., and Cramer, B. G. 1990. *The Earliest Relationship*. New York: Addison-Wesley.

Browning, R. 1973. *The Pied Piper of Hamelin*. New York: Coward, McCann, & Geoghegan.

Bruner, J. 1990. *Acts of Meaning*. Cambridge: Harvard Univ. Press.

Calvino, I. 1974. *Invisible Cities*. W. Weaver, Trans., New York: Harcourt Brace Jovanovich.

————. 1979. *if on a winter's night a traveler*. W. Weaver, Trans., New York: Harcourt Brace Jovanovich.

Chodorow, N. 1978. *The Reproduction of Mothering: Psychoanalysis and the Sociology of Gender*. Berkeley: Univ. of California Press.

Clearly, B. 1975. *Ramona the Brave*. New York: Dell.

Cuban, L. 1993. *How Teachers Taught*. New York: Teacher's College Press.

Cuddihy, J. M. 1974. *The Ordeal of Civility*. New York: Basic Books.

Damasio, A. 1994. *Descartes' Error*. New York: Grosset/Putnam.

deMause, L. 1974. "The Evolution of Childhood." In L. deMause Ed., *The History of Childhood*. New York: The Psychohistory Press.

Dennett, D. 1991. *Consciousness Explained*. Boston: Little, Brown.

Dennison, G. 1969. *The Lives of Children: Story of the First Street School*. New York: Vintage.

Dewey, J. [1902]1956. *The Child and the Curriculum/The School and Society*. Chicago: Univ. of Chicago Press.

————. 1929. *The Quest for Certainty*. New York: Minton, Balch.

————. 1991. *How We Think*. Buffalo, New York: Prometheus.

Dickinson, E. (n.c). *The Complete Poems of Emily Dickinson*. T. H. Johnson Ed. Boston: Little, Brown.

Dylan, B. 1965. "Like a Rolling Stone." In *Highway 61 Revisited*. New York: Columbia Records.

————. 1965. "It's Alright, Ma, I'm Only Bleeding." In *Bringing It All Back Home*. New York: Columbia Records.

————. 1966. "The Ballad of Frankie Lee and Judas Priest." In *John Wesley Harding*. New York: Columbia Records.

Eagleton, T. 1990. *Ideology of the Aesthetic*. Cambridge, England: Basil Blackwell.

Edelman, G. 1992. *Bright Air, Brilliant Fire*. New York: Basic Books.

Eigen, M. 1992. *Coming Through the Whirlwind*. Wilamette, Illinois: Chiron.

Emerson, R. W. 1982. *Emerson in His Journals*. J. Porte, Ed., Cambridge: Harvard Univ. Press.

Erikson, E. H. [1950]1993. *Childhood and Society*. New York: Norton.

Fisher, C. 1992. "Experimental and Clinical Approaches to the Mind-Body Problem through Recent Research in Sleep and Dreaming." In M. R. Lansky Ed., *Essential Papers on Dreams*. New York: New York Univ. Press.

Flax, J. 1990. *Thinking Fragments: Psychoanalysis, Feminism, and Postmodernism in the Contemporary West*. Los Angeles: Univ. of California Press.

Foucault, M. 1979. *Discipline and Punish*. A. Sheridan, Trans. New York: Vintage.

Freeman, M. 1993. *Rewriting the Self*. New York: Routledge & Kegan Paul.

Freeman, W. 1991, February: "The Physiology of Perception." *Scientific American*, 78-85.

Freire, P. [1970]1985. *Pedagogy of the Oppressed*. M. B. Ramos, Trans. New York: Continuum.

Freud, S. 1992. "Revision of Dream Theory." In M. Lansky, Ed., *Essential Papers on Dreams*. New York: New York Univ. Press.

Frost, R. 1967. "Death of the Hired Man." In G. Sanders, J. Nelson, and M. Rosenthal Eds., *Chief Modern Poets of England and America*. New York: Macmillan.

Garbarino, J., Dubrow, N., and Kostelny, K. 1991. *No Place to Be a Child*. Lexington, Massachusetts: Lexington Books.

Garcia, J., and Hunter, R. 1970. "Ripple" on *American Beauty*. New York: Warner Records.

Gardner, H. 1991. *The Unschooled Mind: How Children Think and How Schools Should Teach*. New York: Basic Books.

Gendlin, E. 1987. "A Philosophical Critique of the Concept of Narcissism: The Significance of the Awareness Movement." In D. M. Levin, Ed., *Pathologies of the Modern Self: Postmodern Studies in Narcissism, Schizophrenia, and Depression*. New York: New York Univ. Press.

Gibson, J. J. 1979. *The Ecological Approach to Visual Perception*. Boston: Houghton-Mifflin.

Graff, G. 1995. *Conflicting Paths: Growing Up in America*. Cambridge: Harvard Univ. Press.

Greenson, R. R. 1992. "The Dream in Psychoanalytic Practice." In M. R. Lansky, Ed., *Essential Papers on Dreams*. New York: New York Univ. Press.

Grumet, M. R. 1988. *Bitter Milk*. Amherst: Univ. of Massachusetts Press.

Gutek, G. L. 1991. *An Introduction to American Education*. Prospect Heights, Illinois: Waveland Press.

Hawthorne, N. 1959. *The Scarlet Letter*. New York: Signet Classics.

Heath, S. B. 1982. *Ways with Words*. New York: Cambridge Univ. Press.

Herrnstein, R. J., and Murray, C. 1994. *The Bell Curve*. New York: The Free Press.

Illick, J. 1974. "Anglo-American Child Rearing." In L. deMause, Ed., *The History of Childhood*. New York: Psychohistory Press.

Jardine, D. W. 1988a. "Piaget's Clay and Descartes' Wax." *Educational Theory*, 38(3; Summer): 287-99.

———. 1988b. "There Are Children All Around Us." *J. of Educational Thought*, 22(2A; October): 178-86.

————. 1989. "Play and Hermeneutics: An Exploration of the Bi-Polarities of Mutual Understanding." *J. of Curriculum Theorizing*, 8(2): 23-41.

Karlsen, C. F. 1987. *The Devil in the Shape of a Woman*. New York: Norton.

Katz, M. Editor. 1973. *Education in American History: Readings on the Social Issues*. New York: Praeger Publishers.

————. 1987. *Reconstructing American Education*. Cambridge: Harvard Univ. Press.

Kett, J. 1977. *Rites of Passage*. New York: Basic Books.

Khan, M. M. 1974. *The Privacy of the Self*. New York: International Universities Press.

Kincheloe, J. 1993. *Toward a Critical Politics of Teacher Thinking: Mapping the Postmodern*. Boston: Bergin and Garvey.

————. forthcoming. "Home Alone and Bad to the Bone: The Advent of a Postmodern Childhood." In S. Steinberg and J. Kincheloe, Eds., *Kinderculture*. Boulder, Colorado: Westview Press.

Kliebard, H. M. 1987. *The Struggle for the American Curriculum*. New York: Routledge and Kegan Paul.

Kohn, A. [1986]1992. *No Contest*. Boston: Houghton-Mifflin Company.

Kovel, J. 1987. "Schizophrenic Being and Technocratic Society." In D. M. Levin, Ed., *Pathologies of the Modern Self: Postmodern Studies on Narcissism, Schizophrenia and Depression*. New York: New York Univ. Press.

Kozol, J. 1967. *Death at an Early Age*. Boston: Houghton-Mifflin.

————. 1991. *Savage Inequalities*. New York: Crown.

————. 1995. *Amazing Grace*. New York: Crown.

Kuhn, T. 1970. *The Structure of Scientific Revolutions*. Chicago: Univ. of Chicago Press.

Lansky, M. 1992. "The Legacy of *The Interpretations of Dreams*." In M. Lansky, Ed., *Essential Papers on Dreams*. New York: New York Univ. Press.

Lansky, M. Ed. 1992. *Essential Papers on Dreams*. New York: New York Univ. Press.

Lemieux, M. 1987. *The Pied Piper of Lemieux*. New York: Morrow Junior Books.

Levinas, E. 1994. *Outside the Subject*. M. B. Smith, Trans. Stanford: Stanford Univ. Press.

Lerner, M. 1994. *Jewish Renewal*. New York: HarperPerennial.

Lyman, R. B. Jr. 1974. "Barbarism and Religion." In L. deMause, Ed., *The History of Childhood*. New York: Psychohistory Press.

Mack, J. 1992. "Toward a Theory of Nightmares." In M. R. Lansky Ed., *Essential Papers on Dreams*. New York: New York Univ. Press.

Mann, H. 1969. *Lectures on Education*. New York: Arno.

Marx, K. [1963]1984. *The Eighteenth Brumaire of Louis Bonaparte*. New York: International Universities Press.

Messerli, J. 1972. *Horace Mann*. New York: Knopf.

Milner, M. 1987. *The Suppressed Madness of Sane Men*. London: Tavistock.

————. [1950]1990. *On Not Being Able to Paint*. Madison, Connecticut: International Universities Press.

Morrison, T. 1994. *Playing in the Dark*. Cambridge: Harvard Univ. Press.

Nasaw, D. 1979. *Schooled to Order: A Social History of Public Schooling in the United States*. New York: Oxford Univ. Press.

Olson, D. 1994. *The World on Paper*. New York: Cambridge Univ. Press.

Paul, R. 1990. *Critical Thinking*. Rohnert Park, California: Center for Critical Thinking and Moral Critique.

Perkinson, H. J. 1991. *The Imperfect Panacea*. New York: McGraw-Hill.

Phillips, A. 1993. *On Kissing, Tickling, and Being Bored*. Cambridge: Harvard Univ. Press.

Pinar, W. F. 1975. "Sanity, Madness and the School." In W. F. Pinar, Ed., *Curriculum Theorizing: The Reconceptualists*. Berkeley, California: McCutchan Publishing Corporation.

———. 1991. "Curriculum as Social Psychoanalysis: The Significance of Place." In J. L. Kincheloe and W. F. Pinar, Eds., *Curriculum as Social Psychoanalysis: The Significance of Place*. Albany: State Univ. of New York Press.

———. 1994. *Autobiography, Politics and Sexuality*. New York: Peter Lang.

Pinar, W. and M. Grumet. 1976. *Toward a Poor Curriculum*. Dubuque, Iowa: Kendall/Hunt Publishing Company.

Pirsig, R. 1967. *Zen and the Art of Motorcycle Maintenance*. New York: Bantam.

Postman, N. 1994. *The Disappearance of Childhood*. New York: Vintage.

Purpel, D. 1989. *The Moral and Spiritual Crisis in Education*. Boston: Bergin and Garvey.

———. 1995. "Spirituality and Education: The Difficulty of Making Long-Term Commitments." Paper presented at the Conference on Spirituality and Education. Plainfield, Vermont: Goddard College.

Ravitch, D. 1995. "National Standards and Curriculum Reform." In A. C. Ornstein and L. S. Behar, Eds., *Contemporary Issues in Curriculum*. Boston: Allyn and Bacon.

Reimer, E. 1971. *School Is Dead: Alternatives in Education*. New York: Doubleday.

Rorty, R. 1989. *Contingency, Irony, and Solidarity*. New York: Cambridge Univ. Press.

Sarton, M. (1973). *Journey of a Solitude*. New York: Norton.

Sacks, O. 1985. *The Man Who Mistook His Wife for a Hat*. New York: Simon and Schuster.

———. 1995. *An Anthropologist on Mars*. New York: Knopf.

Shaffer, P. 1973. *Equus*. New York: Penguin.

Silin, J. 1995. *Sex, Death, and the Education of Children*. New York: Teacher's College Press.

Shakespeare, W. 1971. *The Complete Works of Shakespeare*. I. Ribner and G. L. Kittredge, Eds. New York: Ginn.

Smith, D. 1988. "Children and the Gods of War." *The J. of Educational Thought*. 22(2A): 173-77.

Smith, F. 1988. *Understanding Reading*. Hillsdale, New Jersey: Lawrence Erlbaum.

Sommerville, C. J. 1987. *The Rise and Fall of Childhood*. New York: Vintage Books.

Stern, D. N. 1985. *The Interpersonal World of the Infant*. New York: Basic Books.

Stolorow, R. D., and Atwood, G. E. 1992. "Dreams and the Subjective World." In M. Lansky, Ed., *Essential Papers on Dreams*. New York: New York Univ. Press.

Summers, F. 1994. *Object Relations Theories and Psychpathology*. Hillsdale, New Jersey: The Analytic Press.

Sykes, C. 1995. *Dumbing Down Our Kids: Why American Children Feel Good About Themselves but Can't Read, Write or Add*. New York: St. Martin's.

Thoreau, H. D. [1834]1961. *A Week on the Concord and Merrimac Rivers*. New York: Crowell.

———. 1962. *The Journals of Henry David Thoreau*. B. Torrey and F. Terry, Eds. New York: Dover.

———. 1980. *The Natural History Essays*. Salt Lake City, Utah: Peregrine Smith.

Trevarthen, C. 1980. "The Foundations of Intersubjectivity: Development of Interpersonal and Cooperative Understanding in Infants." In D. Olson, Ed., *The Social Foundations of Language*. New York: Norton.

Vonnegut, K. 1969. *Cat's Cradle*. New York: Dell.

Vygotsky, L. 1978. *Mind and Society*. M. Cole et al., Eds. Cambridge: Harvard Univ. Press.

Walzer, J. 1974. "A Period of Ambivalence." In L. deMause, Ed., *A History of Childhood*. New York: Psychohistory Press.

West, C. 1993. *Prophetic Thought in Postmodern Times*. Monroe, Maine: Common Courage.

Willis, G., et al., Editors. 1994. *The American Curriculum: A Documentary History*. Westport, Connecticut: Praeger.

Winnicott, D. W. 1965. *The Maturational Processes and the Facilitating Environment*. New York: International Universities Press, Inc.

———. 1971. *Playing & Reality*. New York: Routledge.

———. 1984. "Aggression and Its Roots." In C. Winnicott, R. Shepherd, and M. Davis, Eds., *Deprivation and Delinquency*. London: Tavistock Publications.

———. 1986. *Home Is Where We Start From*. New York: Norton.

Zuckerman, M. 1973. "Socialization in Colonial New England." In M. Katz, Ed., *Education in American History*. New York: Praeger.

Index